100

THINGS TO DO IN

OHIO

BEFORE YOU

DIE

Thomas Edison's Birthplace
in Milan, Ohio

100

THINGS TO DO IN

OHIO

BEFORE YOU

DIE

· ·

BRANDY GLEASON

REEDY PRESS

Library of Congress Control Number: 2024930387

ISBN: 9781681065175

Design by Jill Halpin

All images are by the author unless otherwise noted.

Printed in the United States of America
24 25 26 27 28   5 4 3

DEDICATION

To all my friends in my Ohio Road Trips Facebook Group
You all are my inspiration to keep writing and sharing all the
wonderful things there are to do in Ohio! Keep road-tripping!

G&R Tavern in Waldo, Ohio

CONTENTS

Music and Entertainment

Sports and Recreation

• •

Culture and History

Shopping and Fashion

Ohio State Parks

PREFACE

Ohio! Go Bucks! The Buckeye State!

Ohio has been my base camp, and I have lived in this great state my whole life. She has kept me busy exploring and enjoying my home state treasures, and at just the right time, she would open up my eyes to something new to see and do.

I am just a small-town girl who loves to explore; Ohio has so many unique places where I can go and feel right at home, walking a revitalized downtown, shopping small and local, then dining in a restaurant that is owned by a winner of a James Beard Award but is off the beaten path.

The beautiful thing about experiencing Ohio is that I have been able to have every kind of vacation, all within the borders of this beautiful place. Beach vacation? Checked off on the shores of Lake Erie. Stays in the woods of southern Ohio with family? Checked off in the unique area of Hocking Hills. While I am always up for a trip out of state, Ohio keeps me coming back for more.

Growing up in a small town in Ohio, I never imagined that one day I would get to write about all the fantastic things to see and do in this great state. From the bustling cities to the quiet countryside, Ohio has something for everyone. As I explore and discover all that Ohio has to offer, I am thrilled to share my experiences with others. So come along with me on this journey, and let's uncover the hidden gems and popular attractions that make Ohio such a special place.

• •

Please share your Ohio adventures with me on your social media! #OhioRoadTrips #100ThingsOhio or join my Ohio Road Trips Facebook group. Tag Gleason Family Adventure and give me a follow on Instagram or Facebook.

Happy road trips!

Brandy Gleason, CTA, ECI

ACKNOWLEDGMENTS

There is never enough ink to fill out this section! I have so many wonderful family, friends, and partners!

I am grateful to the Lord for giving me the gift of writing and the opportunity to share with you all.

My parents: These two wonderful people gave me the passion to explore and travel. Thank you for letting me make homemade rafts with the Lyndaker kids to float downstream, and thanks for coming to find us when we floated too far. I am grateful for the time you took us to Yellowstone National Park and decided to stay the night in the campground even though we did not have a pillow or blanket in the car. The real win was all the campers who gave us stuff to use that night and let us join in the campfire fun; I think this is where my love of camping was cemented. These things instilled a love for adventure, travel, and road-tripping.

My family: Matt, you have given me free rein to go for all the things and just handed over the VISA card when I randomly booked trips. Thank you for being my travel partner; I look forward to retirement adventures with you! To my eight kids, you all have been great to explore with. I have loved creating off-the-chart experiences with you. To the unnamed child, thanks for the trip to Gettysburg National Park; I am glad I could ensure your education was complete before graduating. If you know, you know.

Thank you to Beth Carmicheal, who has pushed me to step out to pursue my career. You are a cheerleader, and for that, I am grateful. Melinda Huntley, you are one of Ohio's biggest advocates. Your ability to educate and teach has impacted me, and I would not be where I am today without OTLA. And no acknowledgments section is complete without saying thank you to Sara Broers for "finding me" and telling me that I was a good writer and should do something with it. You changed my life for the better.

Ohio tourism partners! Thank you for all your help, hospitality, and hard work to make sure I have the correct information and everything is in order. You all are amazing.

• •

The Morgan House in Dublin, Ohio

FOOD AND DRINK

EAT IN A CABIN
FROM THE 1800S

As you approach the Morgan House cabin, you're immediately greeted by its rustic charm. The primitive hand-hewn logs from the 1800s create an authentic atmosphere that transports you back in time. Once you step inside The Morgan House, be sure to put your name on the list at the host stand and ask to be seated in the original cabin. From there, it's time to choose what to have for lunch. The Morgan House soup is a must-try, with its unique blend of flavors that includes a hint of curry. Don't forget to pair it with the flavored coffee of the day and a chicken salad sandwich served on a fresh croissant. And if you have a sweet tooth, the dessert options are sure to please. Christmastime is an especially delightful time to visit, as the whole venue is decorated from top to bottom with sprays of garland and trees filled with ornaments, filling the cabin with merry and bright holiday joy. While you wait for your table, take a leisurely stroll through the 18,000 square feet of shopping space, filled with everything from rustic to modern items. It's the perfect way to pass the time and discover some hidden treasures.

5300 Glick Rd., Dublin, 614-889-5703
morganhse.com

GRAB A STEIN OF BEER
AT SCHMIDT'S

Listen for the polka music as you find your way to Schmidt's Sausage Haus und Restaurant in the German Village neighborhood of Columbus. Schmidt's was founded in 1886 as a meat packing facility by J. Fred Schmidt and became a restaurant in 1967. Schmidt's is known for their wide variety of sausages (which are made fresh daily), schnitzel, house-made sauerkraut, and spaetzle. While these delicious dishes are worth coming out for, the local favorite is the cream puff, a puff pastry filled with a cool, silky filling that is to die for. If you love German food, then this historic stop needs to make your *wunschliste der lebensträume* (wish list of dreams)! Dine where they have been serving up authentic German food for 130 years!

240 E Kossuth St., Columbus, 614-444-6808
schmidthaus.com

TIP
Plan to come during the Columbus Oktoberfest, when lively oompah music fills the beer garden, and the bier taps are flowing.
717 E 17th Ave., Columbus
columbusoktoberfest.com

ENJOY LOCAL BEEF
WITH CHEF-DRIVEN FAST FOOD

Have you ever found that joint where you just know that whenever you are within an hour and a half of the place, you're going to make the drive and eat there no matter what? Well, 360 Burger is that place in Cambridge. Let me tell you, the burgers here are absolutely phenomenal. Maybe it's because the beef is from the cattle they raise on their farm, or because of the locally sourced ingredients they use, but whatever it is, this place is always firing on all cylinders. Add a ginormous helping of fresh-cut fries and you have got the perfect pairing. But wait, there's more! Not only was the burger amazing and the fries aplenty, you will want to try the vanilla bourbon salted caramel milkshake. You read that correctly: a boozy milkshake to give your meal here that over-the-top finish. Got kids? No problem, they serve regular milkshakes, too!

11201 Cadiz Rd., Cambridge, 740-435-0360
the360burger.com

TIP

Looking for something a little more upscale but still farm-to-fork? Their sister restaurant, the Bear's Den Steakhouse, serves the best steaks around.

13320 E Pike Rd., Cambridge, 740-432-5285

bearsdensteakhouse.com

HAVE A BREAKFAST FAVORITE
AT THE FARMER'S DAUGHTER

Urbana is home to the Farmer's Daughter restaurant, a hidden gem my family discovered years ago. It holds a special place in my heart since my Grandpa Stalnaker and I used to frequent it together. Now, I often return to reminisce about my wonderful times with him and indulge in Jenni's delightful home cooking. As you approach the entrance, you'll be greeted by a big red tractor—the perfect spot for a photo op! Inside, the staff will welcome you with a friendly greeting and wave. Don't miss out on ordering one of their famous Hog Logs, a mouthwatering breakfast item filled with crumbled sausage, chunks of bacon and ham, eggs, and cheese, all wrapped up in a flour tortilla and topped with their homemade sausage gravy. They make most everything in-house, including their delectable cinnamon rolls and freshly crafted pies, which will keep you coming back for more, time and time again. Create your own memories here, enjoying the best of Champaign County.

904 Miami St., Urbana, 937-653-3276
thefarmersdaughterllc.com

TRY A WORLD-FAMOUS
TOLEDO HOT DOG SHOP

Tony Packo's in Toledo is a special place for food enthusiasts and those seeking an off-the-charts dining experience. As soon as you step into this establishment, you'll be transported to a vibrant and charming old-world atmosphere lit up with nostalgic Tiffany lamps that will make you feel right at home. However, it's the food that truly sets Tony Packo's apart from any other restaurant you've visited. You absolutely must try their world-renowned Hungarian hot dogs, which are generously topped with their signature chili and a tantalizing blend of cheeses that will have your taste buds bursting with excitement! The sides are just as mouthwatering, featuring hot German potato salads, homemade paprikás dumplings smothered in traditional paprikás gravy, and a dish of practically perfect pickles that are worth the trip alone. But what really makes Tony Packo's stand out is the entire atmosphere of the historic joint. Burt Reynolds was the first celebrity to sign his bun, and now the walls are entirely covered in autographs and memorabilia. Be sure to take some time to peruse them all before you leave.

1902 Front St., Toledo, 419-691-6054
tonypackoscatering.com

OVERLOOK THE FALLS AS YOU DINE
AT CLIFTON MILL RESTAURANT

If you have ever wanted to eat in a restored mill, the Historic Clifton Mill Restaurant offers a distinct and memorable experience. As you walk in, you will be met with rustic beams and exposed walls graced with antique decor. The dining room overlooks the falls, and the sound of rushing water accompanies your dining experience. Each meal is cooked with a flare of country, with some dishes even teetering on upscale. Come during breakfast for one of the plate-sized pancakes. And the desserts, oh the desserts! From homemade pies to decadent cakes, every sweet treat is a delightful indulgence that is worth saving room for. Visit during the holiday season and explore the grounds, which are lit up with an award-winning display of millions of Christmas lights, and you can even have a visit with Santa.

75 Water St., Clifton, 937-767-5501
cliftonmill.com

TIP

After your meal, take a walk at Clifton Gorge
State Nature Preserve, just down the road; it is
one of Eastern Ohio's most scenic hikes.

2381 State Rte. 343, Yellow Springs
ohiodnr.gov/go-and-do/plan-a-visit/find-a-property/
clifton-gorge-state-nature-preserve

INDULGE IN ICE CREAM
AT AN ICONIC DAIRY

Young's Jersey Dairy is a popular Ohioan ice cream tradition that offers an array of fun activities and things to do for families and friends. Beginning with Hap Young's purchase of 60 acres after World War ll, the dairy has a rich history that lives on to this day. The huge ice cream shop at the dairy offers signature flavors, still all made in small batches; I can definitely recommend the peanut butter and chocolate! It is more than ice cream, though; they serve up some killer cheese curds and hearty sandwiches. Once you're there, you'll never want to leave because of the numerous activities available. There are goats to feed, jersey cows to pet, miniature golf to play, and Cowvin's fast slide to slide down. Additionally, Young's Jersey Dairy has a "cowlendar" of events, so plan your ice cream adventure during one of them!

6880 Springfield-Xenia Rd., Yellow Springs, 937-325-0629
youngsdairy.com

TIP

In the fall, the dairy transforms into a pumpkin patch of bright-colored orbs during the autumn festivities, making it an ideal time to visit.

OTHER ICE CREAM SHOPS IN OHIO

Toft's Dairy
Milk is delivered to the Toft's in Sandusky 365 days a year from
13 local farms, all of which are within a 50-mile radius, keeping
the "One Quality" philosophy a tradition that has continued
through five generations.
3717 Venice Rd., Sandusky, 419-625-4376
toftdairy.com

Dietsch Brothers
A Findley favorite since 1937! Locals give this one a thumbs-up and
have said you've got to try one of the seasonal flavors.
400 W Main Cross St., Findlay, 419-422-4486
dietschs.com

Velvet Ice Cream
A Buckeye sensation since 1914. Grab a scoop of one of the 50
flavors and visit Ohio's only ice cream museum. (Open seasonally)
11324 Mt. Vernon Rd., Utica, 740-892-3921
velveticecream.com

Jeni's Splendid Ice Creams
Bursts of unique flavors come alive with every lick of these
bougie cones. Jeni Britton has created an ice cream community
right in the heart of Columbus.
59 Spruce St., Columbus, 614-488-3224
jenis.com

Tom's Ice Cream Bowl
For 70 years, they have brought old-fashioned
heaping bowls of ice cream flavors to happy people.
532 McIntire Ave., Zanesville, 740-452-5267
tomsicecreambowl.com

SAMPLE
THE BEST DOUGHNUTS
IN OHIO

If you're a fan of sweets and are looking for a unique experience in Ohio, the Donut Trail in Butler County should be a road trip you take to get all the good stuff. The trail is a self-guided tour that takes you to some of the best doughnut shops in the area, each offering a distinct flavor and style, with their own specialty. From classic glazed doughnuts to more adventurous flavors like maple bacon, there is something here for everyone. The trail also offers a fun way to explore the quaint towns and villages in Butler County. To participate in the Donut Trail, you'll need to grab a passport booklet from any of the participating shops or the Travel Butler County Visitors Bureau. The booklet features a map of all the stops on the trail and spaces to collect stamps from each shop. Once you've collected stamps from all 12 shops, you can return your passport for a free Donut Trail T-shirt. But the trail isn't just about collecting stamps and free T-shirts; the real reward is the opportunity to taste some of the most delectable doughnuts in the state of Ohio.

Travel Butler County
8756 Union Centre Blvd., West Chester
travelbutlercounty.com/sites/default/files/donut-trail-map.pdf

Central Pastry Shop
1518 Central Ave., Middletown

Holtman's Donuts
9558 Civic Centre Blvd., West Chester

Jupiter Coffee & Donuts
5353 Dixie Hwy., Ste. 5, Fairfield

Kelly's Bakery
1335 Main St., Hamilton

Martin's Donuts
4 W State St., Trenton

Milton's Donuts
3533 Roosevelt Blvd., Middletown

Mimi's Lil' Kitchen
2267 Millville Ave., Hamilton

Oxford Doughnut Shoppe
120 S Locust St., Oxford

Ross Bakery
1051 Eaton Ave., Hamilton
4421 Hamilton Cleves Rd., Hamilton

Stan the Donut Man
7967 Cincinnati Dayton Rd., West Chester

The Donut Dude
7132 Cincinnati Dayton Rd., #1000, Liberty Township

The Donut Hole by Milton's Donuts
8268 Princeton Glendale Rd., West Chester

The Donut Spot
5130 Pleasant Ave., Fairfield

CELEBRATE TRADITION AND FINE DINING
AT THE PINE CLUB

The Pine Club in Dayton is a legendary steak house that has been serving up some of the best cuts of meat in the area for over 70 years. This restaurant has become a staple in the community and is known as a classic dining experience. The Pine Club emanates old-school charm and a cozy and intimate atmosphere that transports you back in time. The walls are adorned with vintage photos and memorabilia, adding to the restaurant's nostalgic feel. But what really sets The Pine Club apart is its steaks. The restaurant features only the finest cuts of USDA Prime beef, aged to perfection and cooked to order. The menu also includes a variety of other dishes, including seafood, salads, and sides, but the steaks are the real star of the show. The signature dish is the "16 oz. Delmonico," a boneless rib eye that is juicy, flavorful, and perfectly cooked every time. Make sure to come hungry and ready to indulge in some of the best steaks in Ohio.

1926 Brown St., Dayton, 937-228-5371
thepineclub.com

TIP
Embracing their long-held traditions, they request proper attire when you join them for dinner.

SINK YOUR TEETH
INTO SMOKIN' HOT BBQ

As soon as you open your car door, the irresistible aroma of the smoker hits you, making your mouth water in anticipation of the delicious smoked meat waiting for you at the Scioto Ribber. This local joint has been serving some of the best barbecue in the small community of Portsmouth, in Southern Ohio, since 1978. The locals swear by it and consider it a place that needs to make your barbecue bucket list. The secret to their mouthwatering flavors lies in the hickory smoke that infuses every bite of their perfectly grilled steaks, tender ribs, and juicy chicken. You won't be able to forget the first succulent bite you take.

1026 Gallia St., Portsmouth, 740-353-9329
thesciotoribber.com

TIP

After satisfying your taste buds at The Scioto Ribber, take a stroll along the Ohio River and discover the stunning Portsmouth Floodwall Murals. This open-air art gallery showcases the area's history over the last two centuries and intrigues art lovers and history buffs alike.
portsmouthmurals.com

DIVE INTO A BOWL OF LOBSTER BISQUE
AT THE BOARDWALK

The Boardwalk and Upper Deck at Put-in-Bay is the perfect spot to kick-start your island adventure. This South Bass Island favorite is renowned for serving up the best seafood on Lake Erie. Don't miss out on their world-famous lobster bisque, which is sure to tantalize your taste buds. The whole property offers panoramic views of the stunning sunsets on the bay from every seat on the deck. Lake Erie is the walleye capital of the world, and you must try their perfectly seasoned fried fish platters served with one of their seasonal sides. Hungry visitors can choose from various dining options on one of the many levels, from upscale table-side service to walk-up counter options. The decks feature multiple bars where you can order a drink and unwind on island time.

341 Bayview Ave., Put-in-Bay, 419-285-3695
the-boardwalk.com

TIP

Ride Miller Ferry or Jet Express over to the island and rent a golf cart to spend the day or weekend exploring the Key West of the Midwest.

Miller Put-in-Bay Ferry
millerferry.com

Jet Express
jet-express.com

CELEBRATE ST. PATRICK'S DAY
RIGHT IN CLEVELAND

When it comes to finding the best corned beef in Cleveland, there's one place that always comes to the top of everyone's mind: Slyman's Restaurant. This iconic deli has been serving up delicious sandwiches since 1963, and it's no surprise that they've become a local pillar for the best ones around. The menu at Slyman's is simple, but everything they serve is made with care and attention to detail. Of course, the star of the show is their corned beef sandwich, which is piled high with tender, juicy meat that practically melts in your mouth, quite literally. The rye bread is always fresh and perfectly toasted, and the sandwich is served with a side of crispy crinkle fries or homemade coleslaw. But don't just take my word for it; this historic deli is one to try.

3106 St. Clair Ave., Cleveland, 216-621-3760
slymans.com

TIP

Lines at Slyman's can be long, especially during peak hours and on St. Patrick's Day, but locals and visitors agree it's worth the wait.

ELEVATE YOUR DINING EXPERIENCE
AT A REGAL CASTLE AMID THE WOODLANDS

Nestled deep within the lush Mohican Forest lies the enchanting Copper Mug Bar & Grille, located on the expansive grounds of Landoll's Mohican Castle. The journey to this hidden gem is a magical one as you traverse the rolling hills that lead up to the entrance. Upon arrival, you'll find the restaurant's parking area situated just below the castle itself. The Copper Mug is a haven for food lovers, serving up three delectable meals a day as well as a fantastic happy hour. Popular lunchtime dishes include the sumptuous table-side-served lobster bisque, the mouthwatering baked brie with crostini, and the hearty two-handed sandwiches. For a more upscale dining experience, make sure to dress up a little in the evening and indulge in the exquisite flavors of the perfectly cooked Angus rib eye or the tantalizing Schnitzel Landoll.

561 Township Rd. 3352, Loudonville, 419-994-3427
landollsmohicancastle.com/dine

TIP
To make this a perfect outing, consider booking a stay in the castle and revel in the grandeur of this regal establishment.

SAVOR HISTORY
IN THE OLDEST CONTINUOUSLY OPERATED BUSINESS IN OHIO

The Golden Lamb Restaurant is truly an extraordinary retreat; from the moment you park your car here, you know you are in for something special. The historic building that houses the restaurant is a sight to behold, with its charming architecture and traditional decor. The atmosphere inside is warm and inviting, with a cozy and intimate feel that makes it perfect for a romantic dinner or a special occasion with friends and family. The menu at The Golden Lamb is perfection, with a mix of classic American dishes and more modern cuisine. Dishes are expertly prepared, with generous portions and a focus on fresh, high-quality ingredients. Some of the standout dishes include the lamb chops, which are tender and flavorful, and the chef's special of fried chicken. Book a room in the Grant Suite and stay for the night as many presidents and dignitaries have in the past, and soak in the history.

27 S Broadway, Lebanon, 513-932-5065
goldenlamb.com

TIP

If you stay overnight, visit the Harmon Museum, explore Lebanon, and ride the Lebanon Mason & Monroe train.

Harmon Museum

105 S Broadway, Lebanon, 513-932-1817

wchsmuseum.org/harmonmuseum.html

Lebanon Mason & Monroe Railroad

16 E South St., Lebanon, 513-933-8022

lebanonrr.com

SIP YOUR WAY THROUGH
OHIO'S WINE COUNTRY

If you're looking for a beautiful wine-country experience, look no further than Ohio's Grand River Valley. Just off the stunning shores of Lake Erie, this area boasts more than 30 wineries and endless vineyards. The rich history of the region is just as rich as the soil itself: thousands of years ago, glaciers formed the Great Lakes and left behind a fertile landscape ideal for grape growing. Today, the unique microclimate of the area and the slopes and valleys that move air and drain water make it the perfect place to grow grapes with deep, complex flavors. The region is responsible for more than 50 percent of Ohio's grapes, and it's easy to see why. Whether you're a lover of cabernet, Riesling, or Vidal, you'll find something to delight your taste buds here. Plan a weekend and book one of the wine tours of the region, and relax and rejuvenate among the wineries.

Grand River Valley
visitashtabulacounty.com

Ferrante Winery & Ristorante
5585 State Rte. 307, Geneva, 440-466-8466
ferrantewinery.com

Grand River Cellars
5750 S Madison Rd./Rte. 528, Madison, 440-298-9838
grandrivercellars.com

Harpersfield Vineyard
6387 State Rte. 307, Geneva, 440-466-4739
harpersfield.com

Largest Estate Winery in Ohio
Debonné Vineyards
7840 Doty Rd., Madison, 440-466-3485

M Cellars
6193 S River Rd. W, Geneva, 440-361-4104
mcellars.com

UNLEASH YOUR INNER FOODIE
AT ODD FODDER

Odd Fodder is an absolute gem that promises a whimsical dining experience like no other. Stepping into this delightful eatery is akin to entering a fantastical world where culinary creativity knows no bounds. The moment you walk through the door, your senses are instantly captivated by the vibrant and eclectic decor. Quirky wall art, mismatched furniture, and a kaleidoscope of colors create an atmosphere that exudes warmth and playfulness. The inviting aroma of delectable dishes wafts through the air, piquing your curiosity and making your taste buds tingle with anticipation. Odd Fodder prides itself on its imaginative menu, where traditional flavors are reimagined and given a delightful twist. From their signature Chicken and Waffle to the mouthwatering mega Odd Shakes, every dish is a work of art that surprises and delights. The culinary masterminds behind Odd Fodder constantly push the boundaries of flavor combinations, using locally sourced, fresh ingredients to ensure the highest quality.

26520 N Dixie Hwy. A, Perrysburg, 419-386-9800
oddfodder.com

DINE IN THE BASEMENT
OF AN OLD CHURCH

Strolling through the imposing gates protected by majestic lions, you'll find yourself transported to a bygone era at Father John's. The restaurant's catacombs are explorable, and the owners encourage your adventuring through their obscure artifacts. Once you've had your fill of the interesting surroundings, settle in at one of the tables and browse the menu. Pick from delectable bison burgers that come from a farm just across the Ohio border in Indiana or one of the mainstay staples. The seasonal menu is always locally sourced and changes with the passing seasons, so be sure to visit often. In the summertime, the enchanting courtyard comes alive with lively music and a festive atmosphere with jovial merrymakers creating a sense of renaissance. Raise your stein of beer and give a cheer while you enjoy your dinner inside this fascinating and restored 19th-century church.

301 W Butler St., Bryan, 419-633-1313

QUENCH YOUR APPETITE
WITH BURGER BLISS

Located in the heart of Lima, Kewpee Hamburgers is a nostalgic burger joint that has delighted locals and visitors alike since 1928. As you step inside, you are immediately transported back in time with its retro decor and old-fashioned charm. The interior of Kewpee is adorned with vintage photographs, Kewpie dolls, and classic memorabilia, creating an atmosphere that is reminiscent of a bygone era. The walls are filled with stories and memories, giving the place a sense of history and character. The menu at Kewpee is centered on their famous burgers, which are made with fresh, never-frozen ground beef and cooked to perfection. As you take your first bite, you are greeted with a burst of flavor that is both juicy and satisfying. The burgers are topped with a secret sauce that adds a tangy and unique twist, making them truly memorable.

Kewpee in Lima is a beloved local institution that combines delicious food, nostalgic ambiance, and friendly service. Whether you're a regular customer or a first-time visitor, you are guaranteed to leave with a full stomach and a smile on your face.

111 N Elizabeth St., Lima, 419-228-1778
kewpeehamburgers.com

OTHER BURGER JOINTS IN OHIO

Crabill's Hamburger Shoppe
727 Miami St., Urbana, 937-653-5133
crabillburgers.com

Swenson's Drive-In
7 locations in Northeast Ohio and two in Central Ohio
swensonsdriveins.com

The Thurman Cafe
183 Thurman Ave., Columbus, 614-443-1570
thethurmancafe.com

Hamburger Wagon
12 E Central Ave., Miamisburg, 937-847-2442
hamburgerwagon.com

ORDER
THE WORLD'S BEST
BOLOGNA SANDWICH

If you are looking for a hole-in-the-wall in the middle of nowhere that is home to the world-famous thick-sliced bologna sandwich, G&R Tavern in Waldo is where you need to point the nose of your car. Upon arrival, you may feel like you're lost in a small town, but don't worry—just park your car by the big sign and head inside. The friendly staff will welcome you warmly, with a hearty call to "Find yourself a seat, and we will be right with you." Everything here is pub food, and the menu is simple: order what you came for, that mouthwatering bologna sandwich. Covered with house-made pickles and a thick slice of onion, this two-handed sandwich will have you singing hallelujah! But that is not all; the mile-high cream pies are the way to finish off this delectable bologna meal.

103 N Marion St., Waldo, 740-726-9685
gandrtavern.com

FEAST AT THE LAST YORK STEAK HOUSE
IN THE COUNTRY

From the moment you walk in and see the picture menu on the wall to when you plop the silverware on the tray and make your way to order, the 1970s feels will overwhelm you. Trust me, it still looks just like it did when I was a kid ordering the chopped steak, thinking I was the queen of it all. Pricing is still great with families in mind. Since 1966, they have been serving high-quality steaks, seafood, and chicken; the sirloin tips or the one-pound T-bone steak are fan favorites! Ask for a side of the mushroom gravy to remember the flavor of childhood. All the desserts are still homemade and freshly prepared; the coconut cream and pumpkin pie are some of the best.

4220 W Broad St., Columbus, 614-272-6485
york-steakhouse.com

TIP

After your meal, visit the Hollywood Casino just a few miles down the road.

200 Georgesville Rd., Columbus, 614-308-3333
hollywoodcolumbus.com

Rock & Roll Hall of Fame in Cleveland, Ohio

MUSIC
AND ENTERTAINMENT

DISCOVER
THE OHIO STATE FAIR

Walking through the gates of the Ohio State Fair is one of the best summertime thrills. All your senses are hit as you hear "Welcome to the Ohio State Fair!" booming over the loudspeaker, wafting smells of funnel cakes and fresh french fries beckoning you in. The Ohio State Fair has been a family tradition since 1850 and continues to be an iconic summer event. No trip to the fair is complete until you see the butter cow sculptures while you eat ice cream from Ohio dairy farmers. If it's a hot day, the Ohio Department of Natural Resources area has green space to enjoy the shade, learn more about Ohio's state parks, and see some of Ohio's native plants and animals. Kids and kids at heart love the barns filled with animals, highlighting the best of Ohio's agriculture. March with the All-Ohio State Fair Youth Choir and Band to round out a day at the fair.

717 E 17th Ave., Columbus
ohiostatefair.com

ROCK OUT
IN CLEVELAND

Head to northern Ohio and plan a visit to jam out at the Rock & Roll Hall of Fame. State-of-the-art exhibits wait to thrill and engage you in the history of rock and roll and enamor you with displays filled with historical memorabilia. Every exhibit within the museum is filled with detailed information; don't leave before taking the time to search out John Mellencamp's motorcycle and Johnny Cash's Fender acoustic guitar. Plan your time at the museum wisely due to the plethora of things to see. Before leaving, make sure to head to the garage to learn how to play your favorite instruments, from a full drum set to electric guitars. If hunger strikes while exploring, no worries; they have a fresh café where you can grab a snack.

1100 Rock and Roll Blvd., Cleveland, 216-781-7625
rockhall.com

TIP
Just outside the Rock & Roll Hall of Fame is one of the iconic Cleveland script signs; take a selfie before you leave.

EXPERIENCE THRILLS
AT THE ROLLER COASTER
CAPITAL OF THE WORLD

Cedar Point is more than a theme park; it is a destination for freshwater beach lovers, history buffs wanting to stay in an old hotel, and golfers wanting to tee off at a resort. In 1870, Cedar Point opened as a public bathing beach, and the first passengers arrived at Cedar Point Resort on the steamer *Young Reindeer.* Now, it is considered a roller coaster mecca, and guests come from around the world for a day in the park. Thrills await visitors on the plethora of heart-racing rides, plus Camp Snoopy is ready for the youngest adventure seekers. Book an extra day to play in the Cedar Point Shores Waterpark, 18 acres of water fun in which to splish-splash the hours away in the summer sun. Slow down a little and enjoy the beach, where you can sit back and relax in the sun, listening to the waves off of Lake Erie with a drink in hand.

1 Cedar Point Dr., Sandusky, 419-627-2350
cedarpoint.com

OTHER THEME PARKS AND WATER PARKS

Kings Island
6300 Kings Island Dr., Kings Island, 513-754-5700
visitkingsisland.com

Great Wolf Lodge
2501 Great Wolf Dr., Mason, 800-913-9653
greatwolf.com/mason

Kalahari
7000 Kalahari Dr., Sandusky, 877-525-2427
kalahariresorts.com/ohio

Zoombezi Bay
4850 W Powell Rd., Powell, 614-645-3400
zoombezibay.com

GET WILD
AT THE COLUMBUS ZOO

The Columbus Zoo and Aquarium is an incredible destination that every animal lover should experience at least once. With the wide range of exhibits and animals on display, you'll never run out of things to see and explore. Make sure to visit the Heart of Africa exhibit, where you can marvel at the majestic giraffes, zebras, cheetahs, and lions. To get the most out of your visit, consider an all-inclusive pass that gives you access to everything, from thrilling rides to the relaxing train ride through the North America exhibit. There are also exciting opportunities to enjoy, such as spending time with Frankie the elephant or taking a night hike with a zookeeper. And don't forget to pack your swimsuit if you're visiting in the summer, and add a day at Zoombezi Bay, where you can enjoy thrilling waterslides and a wave pool then soak up the sun.

4850 W Powell Rd., Powell, 614-645-3400
columbuszoo.org

TIP
Over the Christmas holiday, the zoo comes alive with brilliant festive lights, Santa, and mugs of hot cocoa.

OTHER ZOOS IN OHIO

Cincinnati Zoo & Botanical Garden
Meet Fiona the Hippo or catch one of
the Wings of Flight shows.
3400 Vine St., Cincinnati, 513-281-4700
cincinnatizoo.org

Cleveland Metroparks Zoo
Experience the Asian Lantern Festival or zip through the sky.
3900 Wildlife Way, Cleveland, 216-661-6500
clevelandmetroparks.com/zoo

Akron Zoo
Themed exhibits and animal encounters await you.
505 Euclid Ave., Akron, 330-375-2550
akronzoo.org

Toledo Zoo
Play in the splash pad, experience
an animal encounter, or ride a zip line!
2 Hippo Way, Toledo, 419-385-5721
toledozoo.org

LINGER AND SOAK IN
THE ART OF THE BUTLER

The Butler Institute of American Art in Youngstown is the crown jewel of the city. The museum building is a masterpiece of architectural beauty, with ornate columns, intricate carvings, and a grand staircase leading you to the main galleries. As you wander through the galleries, you can't help but be mesmerized by the museum's ambiance. Soft lighting, elegant decor, and tranquil music create a serene atmosphere, inviting visitors to linger and soak in the beauty surrounding them. One of the museum's standout features is its American Impressionist collection, which boasts works by renowned artists like Winslow Homer, including his impressive piece *Snap the Whip*. In addition to the art collections, the Butler Institute offers educational programs and events for visitors of all ages. If you're looking for a unique and enriching cultural experience, the Butler Institute is not to be missed; it's no wonder the museum is a beloved institution in the Youngstown community.

524 Wick Ave., Youngstown, 330-743-1107
butlerart.com

SING ALONG
WITH THE ENTERTAINERS
AT A DINNER THEATER

Look no further than La Comedia Dinner Theatre in Springboro for a truly enchanting evening. With a rich history of over 45 years, they have consistently delivered one-of-a-kind live performances to their dinner guests. Treat yourself to their "Ohio famous" hot buffet, where you can indulge in their signature house salad topped with their mouthwatering papaya chutney dressing. Once you have finished your meal, sit back and prepare to be amazed by the talented performers who will take the stage. From live music to hilarious comedy and awe-inspiring acrobatics, whatever style of a show being featured is sure to keep you captivated from start to finish. Whether you prefer breathtaking acts, darling dances, or beautiful ballads, La Comedia Dinner Theatre has something for everyone to enjoy. Celebrate a special occasion with them because they will make it memorable.

765 W Central Ave., Springboro, 937-746-4554
lacomedia.com

TIP

Book your tickets well in advance during the Christmas holiday; they sell out quickly.

WATCH THE STARS UNDER THE STARS
AT ELM ROAD DRIVE-IN THEATRE

Have you ever experienced the magic of a nostalgic drive-in movie theater? If not, then you're in for a treat! Picture this: a warm summer night, stars twinkling above, and the sound of crickets chirping in the background. You're sitting comfortably in your car, surrounded by friends or family, and watching a classic movie on a big screen. The smell of freshly buttered popcorn wafts through the air, and everyone is in high spirits, excited to be out and about. That is what you will find at Elm Road Triple Drive-In Theatre in Warren. This family-owned-and-operated drive-in has been showcasing Hollywood's greatest films and stars on the big screen for over 70 years. Be sure to arrive early to order dinner from their newly renovated concession stand.

1895 Elm Rd. NE, Warren, 330-372-9732
elmroadtripledrivein.com

TIP
They are cash-only for movie ticket purchases, so make sure you have money; the concession stand takes cash and card.

OTHER DRIVE-INS IN OHIO

Skyview Drive-In Theatre
2420 E Main St., Lancaster, 740-653-5517
skyviewdrivein.com

Lynn Drive-In Movies
9735 State Rte. 250 NW, Strasburg, 330-878-5797
lynndrivein.com

Blue Sky Drive-In Theater
959 Broad St., Wadsworth, 330-334-1809
blueskydrive-in.com

Holiday Auto Theatre
1816 Old Oxford Rd., Hamilton, 513-929-2999
holidayautotheatre.com

Melody 49 Drive-In Theatre
7606 Pleasant Plain Rd., Brookville, 937-833-5015
melody49drivein.com

South Drive-In Theatre
3050 S High St., Columbus, 614-491-6771
drive-inmovies.com

SEE NATURE
THROUGH A NEW PERSPECTIVE

Love nature? The Holden Arboretum is a breathtaking natural haven that boasts over 3,600 acres of preserved land, making it one of the largest arboretums in the United States. This beautiful destination is ideal for nature lovers to explore and experience the great outdoors in a serene and peaceful setting. Visitors to the Holden Arboretum can enjoy a wide variety of outdoor activities such as hiking, bird-watching, and picnicking. It is home to an impressive collection of plant life, including more than 120,000 trees, shrubs, and other plants from around the world. Take time to visit the butterfly garden, the hedge collection, and the rhododendron garden; they are impeccably curated. Holden Arboretum is unique, with the Emergent Tower which offers stunning views of the surrounding landscape from its observation deck at the top, and the Canopy Walk. This 500-foot-long elevated walkway takes visitors through the tree canopy for a unique perspective on the landscape. Whether you're a seasoned outdoors enthusiast or just looking for a peaceful retreat, the Holden Arboretum is sure to leave a lasting impression.

9550 Sperry Rd., Kirtland, 440-946-4400
holdenfg.org

TIP
Take the tram ride through the arboretum if you are short on time or have difficulty walking.

MARVEL AT THE SPLENDOR
OF THE OHIO THEATRE

The Ohio Theatre is one of the most iconic and historic theaters in the United States. Located in downtown Columbus, the theater has been a staple of the community for over 90 years. Built in 1928, the Ohio Theatre was originally designed as a movie palace and was one of the first theaters in the country to feature sound. Today, the theater welcomes theatergoers to concerts, Broadway shows, and other live performances, with *The Nutcracker* being a holiday favorite. Stunning architecture and ornate design make it an unprecedented stop. The theater's interior is adorned with intricate details and features a grand staircase, crystal chandeliers, and a 21-foot-high ceiling; take time to let your eyes drink it all in. The theater also boasts a Wurlitzer organ, which is one of only a few remaining in the country. Over the years, the Ohio Theatre has played host to some of the biggest names in entertainment, including Elvis Presley, Frank Sinatra, and the Rolling Stones. Today, the Ohio Theatre is home to the Columbus Symphony, BalletMet, and Broadway in Columbus, and the theater continues to be a beloved cultural institution in the Columbus community and by all Ohioans.

39 E State St., Columbus, 614-469-0939
capa.com/venues/detail/ohio-theatre

GET AWAY
TO THE ITALIAN-INSPIRED GERVASI VINEYARD

Gervasi Vineyard is a one-of-a-kind winery experience in Northeast Ohio surrounded by lush vineyards. Known for its stunning Italian-inspired architecture and peaceful ambiance, this winery calls all wine enthusiasts and travelers alike. The vineyard boasts a range of award-winning wines that are crafted using traditional European winemaking techniques. In addition to its exquisite wines, Gervasi Vineyard also features a range of dining options to suit every palate. The Bistro offers a casual and laid-back atmosphere, where guests can enjoy wood-fired pizzas, handcrafted sandwiches, and other delicious dishes. For a more upscale dining experience, make a reservation at the Crush House, which serves up a delectable selection of small plates, entrées, and desserts. Whether you're looking for a romantic getaway, a girls' spa getaway, or a fun-filled outing with friends and family, Gervasi Vineyard should make the top of your list. With its stunning scenery, live music, world-class wines, and exceptional dining options, this winery is sure to leave a lasting impression on all who visit.

1700 55th St. NE, Canton, 330-497-1000
gervasivineyard.com

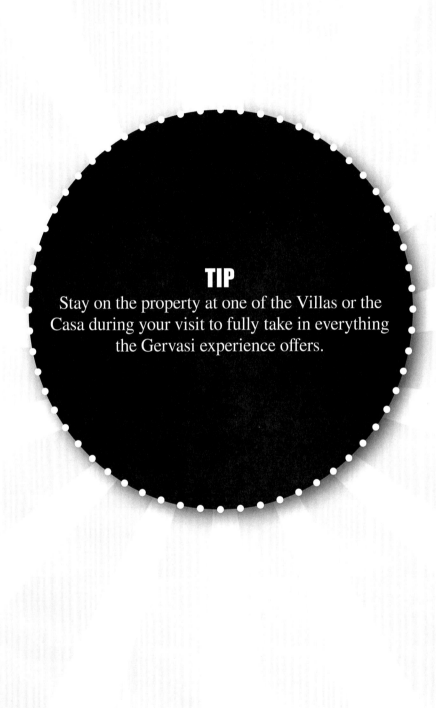

TIP
Stay on the property at one of the Villas or the Casa during your visit to fully take in everything the Gervasi experience offers.

GO BACK IN TIME
WITH A DRIVE DOWN THE STRIP
AT GENEVA-ON-THE-LAKE

The Strip at Geneva-on-the-Lake is a mile-long step back in time that has something to offer for every age group. This iconic Ohio summer destination is home to a variety of attractions, restaurants, and shops that cater to different tastes and interests. The Strip will impress you whether you're a fan of vintage charm, outdoor activities, or local history. One of the most popular spots on the Strip is Eddie's Grill, a timeless diner serving delicious burgers and shakes since 1950. With its old-fashioned decor and friendly staff, Eddie's is the perfect place to grab a quick bite and soak up the retro atmosphere. Families love Adventure Zone—an entertainment complex that boasts go-karts, mini golf, batting cages, and an arcade—and Lake Erie Canopy Tours to fly through the sky on zip lines. For those who prefer a more laid-back experience, the Strip offers several wineries and breweries where you can sample local wines and beers while taking in the scenic lake views.

Geneva-on-the-Lake Convention and Visitors Bureau
440-275-3203
visitgenevaonthelake.com

TIP
Rent a golf cart to zip through the Strip and find parking more accessible.

Eddie's Grill
5377 Lake Rd. E, Geneva-on-the-Lake
440-466-8720
eddiesgrill.com

Adventure Zone Family Fun Center
5600 Lake Rd. E, Geneva-on-the-Lake
440-466-3555
adventurezonefun.com

Lake Erie Canopy Tours
4888 N Broadway/State Rd. 534, Geneva-on-the-Lake
866-601-1973
lakeeriecanopytours.com

ENJOY A SHOW
AT THE LONGEST CONTINUOUSLY RUNNING OPERA HOUSE IN OHIO

The Twin City Opera House is a historic landmark located in McConnelsville, built in 1892; it has been an important cultural center for the area ever since. The opera house has a rich history, having played host to a wide range of events over the years, including plays, concerts, dances, and more. One of the most notable features of the Twin City Opera House is its stunning architecture. The building boasts a beautiful brick exterior and an ornate interior that is filled with intricate details. The opera house has been carefully restored over the years to ensure that it remains a vibrant and vital part of the community. Today, the Twin City Opera House continues to be a popular destination for locals and visitors alike. It regularly hosts various events, including live music, theater productions, and movie nights. The Twin City Opera House is a true shining gem of southern Ohio. It should make the bucket list for anyone interested in history, culture, and the arts—and the paranormal seekers.

15 W Main St., McConnelsville, 740-675-5342
twincityoperahouse.com

BE ENTHRALLED
WITH THE EPIC TALE OF TECUMSEH AT THE OUTDOOR THEATER

The Tecumseh! at the Sugarloaf Mountain Amphitheatre in Chillicothe is a place where lovers of theater and history collide. The drama is named after the great Native American warrior Tecumseh, who fought for the independence of his people against the encroachment of White settlers. The theater is an impressive structure, with seating for more than 1,700 people and a stage over 100 feet wide. The productions that take place here are nothing short of spectacular, with a cast of over 100 actors, dancers, and musicians bringing the story of Tecumseh to life. You can't stop yourself from feeling your heart beat as it tells the story of Tecumseh's struggle against the White settlers and the British and his eventual defeat at the Battle of Tippecanoe. The production is an epic tale of bravery, sacrifice, and love, with stunning visual effects, thrilling battle scenes, and a moving musical score.

5968 Marietta Rd., Chillicothe, 866-775-0700
tecumsehdrama.com

TIP
Purchase a VIP ticket to get the complete package for the night.

JOURNEY TO A PLACE
WHERE HISTORY AND FANTASY BECOME ONE

The Ohio Renaissance Festival is a beloved annual event that transports visitors back in time to the 16th century. Held in Waynesville, the festival features a variety of attractions, activities, and performances that celebrate the era of knights, nobles, and adventurers. One of the many highlights of the festival is the jousting tournament, where brave knights on horseback compete in thrilling competitions of skill and bravery. Enjoy live music, comedy shows, and street performances that showcase the talents of actors, musicians, and performers from around the world. No trip to the Ren Fest would be complete without a hearty turkey leg, savory pastries, and refreshing ale. Browse through the artisan marketplace to find handmade crafts, jewelry, and other unique treasures. For those who want to fully immerse themselves in the Renaissance experience, the festival offers a costume contest and a variety of workshops and classes on topics such as sword fighting, archery, and calligraphy. The Ren Fest is an unforgettable experience that offers a glimpse into a bygone era of chivalry, adventure, and romance. Whether you're a history buff, a fan of fantasy, or just looking for a fun and unique way to spend a day, the festival is sure to delight and entertain.

10542 Ohio 73, Waynesville, 513-897-7000
renfestival.com

OTHER GREAT OHIO FESTIVALS

Ohio River Sternwheel Festival
sternwheel.org

Circleville Pumpkin Show
pumpkinshow.com

Grand Rapids Applebutter Fest
applebutterfest.org

Ashtabula Covered Bridge Festival
coveredbridgefestival.org

Bucyrus Bratwurst Festival
bucyrusbratwurstfestival.com

The Ohio Swiss Festival
ohioswissfestival.com

Hocking Hills Bigfoot Festival
hockinghillsbigfoot.com

FEEL CHRISTMAS SPIRIT
YEAR-ROUND

Step inside Castle Noel, and you'll find yourself immersed in a whimsical realm filled with dazzling lights, festive decorations, and an incredible collection of Christmas memorabilia.

One of the highlights of Castle Noel is its impressive collection of movie props and costumes from beloved Christmas films. You can marvel at the original Grinch sleigh, get up close to the actual Santa suits worn by Hollywood legends, or even take a stroll through millions of dollars of animated New York City Christmas windows from Sak's Fifth Avenue, Lord & Taylor, Bloomingdales, and more.

But Castle Noel isn't just about movie magic. It also offers an array of interactive exhibits and activities that will delight visitors of all ages. Explore the Blizzard Vortex—a simulated winter storm experience that will leave you in awe. Laugh your way through the Santa Klaus Chimney Squeeze, the official training center of Santa, and slide down the Giant Red Slide, just like Ralphie in *A Christmas Story*. Don your Santa hats, and get ready to be transported to a world where Christmas dreams do still come true. Castle Noel awaits, ready to offer you an unforgettable journey into the magic of the holiday season.

260 S Court St., Medina, 330-721-6635
castlenoel.com

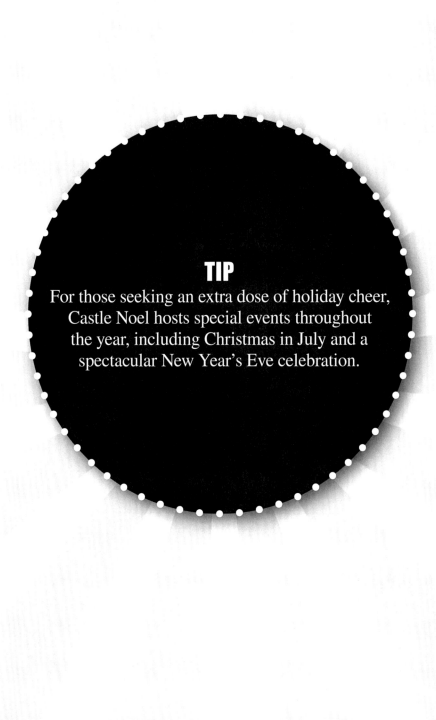

TIP

For those seeking an extra dose of holiday cheer, Castle Noel hosts special events throughout the year, including Christmas in July and a spectacular New Year's Eve celebration.

GAZE
AT THE STUNNING TUDOR REVIVAL ARCHITECTURE OF STAN HYWET HALL

Stan Hywet Hall & Gardens in Akron is a stunning example of Tudor Revival architecture and is considered one of the finest examples of this style in the United States. Built in the early 20th century by F. A. Seiberling, cofounder of the Goodyear Tire & Rubber Company, the estate features a 65-room manor house, beautiful gardens, and several other buildings on the expansive grounds. The hall is a popular attraction for tourists and locals alike, offering guided tours of the house and gardens, as well as special events throughout the year. The house is filled with original furnishings and artwork, giving visitors a glimpse into the life of the Seiberling family and their luxurious lifestyle. The gardens, designed by renowned landscape architect Warren H. Manning, are beautiful, featuring a variety of flowers, trees, and shrubs in a naturalistic setting. Words cannot adequately express the magnificence; you must see it for yourself!

714 N Portage Path, Akron, 330-836-5533
stanhywet.org

TIP
There are multiple tours to choose from; do your research in advance.

PLAY
NOSTALGIC PINBALL MACHINES

Past Times Arcade, one of Ohio's newest retro-themed arcades, has more than 600 pinball and classic arcade games to choose from. You might be surprised when you walk in and see all the machines neatly lined up, ready for you to play. Pay for the one-time play fee for the day and get ready for an evening of good old-fashioned fun. Run your hands over iconic wooden pinball machines that have been meticulously restored and are now ready for you to play. Playing pinball will exhilarate and challenge you since it combines skill, reflexes, and strategy, with the satisfying clinks and dings of the machine along with the flashing lights and unpredictable bounces; it creates thrilling and high-energy play. This nostalgic pastime always brings joy and excitement to beginners and seasoned players alike. Grab a hand-spun milkshake in between games at the '50s-themed diner.

419 N State St., Girard, 330-765-4121
pasttimesarcade.com

TAKE A ROAD TRIP
TO THE SWEET TASTE OF MAPLE SYRUP

There's nothing quite like the sweet, rich taste of maple syrup. Whether you're pouring it over pancakes or using it as a glaze for meats, the distinct flavor of this natural sweetener is sure to please your taste buds. Plan a road trip down country roads to visit the maple syrup sugar shacks peppered throughout the counties in Northeast Ohio. From February into March, the maple sap flows through the tubes going from tree to tree into the buckets, waiting to make the maply deliciousness. At the sugar shacks you'll find every grade of maple syrup, candies, cotton candy, and maple syrup sugar to flavor your coffee. Do your research because while you are here, you'll want to pick a place to have a pancake breakfast on one of the farms or local restaurants. Stop in Burton at the visitor center for a maple syrup tasting if you don't have time for a pancake breakfast.

Maple Madness® Driving Trail listing of all the sugar shacks to stop at
ohiomaple.org/maple-madness.html

TIP

If you're looking for a unique experience, head to the Geauga County Maple Festival, where the end of the maple syrup season is celebrated and championed. It's definitely worth the trip!

440-332-7055
maplefestival.com

ENTERTAIN THE KIDS
WHILE THEY LEARN

Prepare to embark on an exciting adventure at Center of Science and Industry, the premier science museum in Columbus! This popular attraction offers a wealth of interactive exhibits and educational experiences catering to visitors of all ages. COSI has something for everyone, from the wonders of space, energy, technology, and the human body to the specially designed Little Kids Space, where your young ones can discover and learn at their level. One of the standout features of COSI is the state-of-the-art planetarium, where you can immerse yourself in a breathtaking journey through the universe. As you enter the ocean exhibit, you'll be greeted by Poseidon, the Greek god of the sea, who stands guard at the entrance. Here, you can play in the water, creating dams and riverways of fun. For a bird's-eye view of everything below, buckle up and bike the high wire, a thrilling experience that is not to be missed. COSI also features special exhibits that change periodically, live shows and demonstrations, and a dedicated area for young learners.

333 W Broad St., Columbus, 614-228-2674
cosi.org

TIP
Make sure to do the hair-raising experience with static electricity.

SLEEP IN A TENT
ON THE GREAT MIAMI RIVER

Looking for a summer camping experience that's out of the ordinary? Look no further than Float Troy! This unique adventure allows you to stay in a floating Smithfly shoal tent anchored on the Great Miami River in Miami County. On select weekends, campers paddle out to their tents for the night and set up camp right in the middle of the river. It's a bit of a challenge to get everything to and into the tent, so pack light. Once you're settled in, you can enjoy playing games, watching the sunset on the water, and waking up to the gentle lapping of the river against the bottom of your tent. And don't worry about bathroom breaks—just paddle to the shore or bring along a port-a-potty.

409 N Elm St., Troy, 937-703-5397
float-troy.com

TIP
Have dinner at the Smith's Boathouse near Treasure Island Park for excellent water views and fantastic food.
439 N Elm St., Troy, 937-335-3837
smithsboathouse.com

Walleye Fishing in Port Clinton, Ohio/Lake Erie

SPORTS
AND RECREATION

IMMERSE YOURSELF IN OHIO STATE PARKS
AT THE LODGES

Ohio is a true haven for nature enthusiasts, boasting some of the most breathtaking state parks in the country. With a whopping 75 state parks to choose from, there's no shortage of options. However, 10 of these parks stand out with their cozy lodges that offer a national park–like feel. By visiting all of them, you'll be treated to some of Ohio's most stunning flora and fauna, majestic waterfalls, and sprawling views of Lake Erie. Each state park with a lodge has something unique to offer, whether it's boating on a glittering lake, hiking through rigorous trails, enjoying fireworks in July, experiencing haunted rooms, or exploring the "Little Smokies." After all your outdoor adventures, be sure to make a reservation at one of the lodges' restaurants to cap off your time in the parks.

TIP

If you're looking for the ultimate state park experience, look no further than Hocking Hills State Park. Widely regarded as the crown jewel of Ohio's state parks, Hocking Hills offers some of the best hiking in the state. And with the recent opening of a beautiful lodge in 2022, Hocking Hills is an absolute must-visit for anyone looking to tick off items from their bucket list.

Burr Oak State Park Lodge
10660 Burr Oak Lodge Rd., Glouster
stayburroak.com

Deer Creek State Park Lodge
22300 State Park Rd. 20, Mt. Sterling
deercreekparklodge.com

Hocking Hills State Park Lodge
20020 State Rte. 664 S, Logan
hockinghillsparklodge.com

Hueston Woods State Park Lodge
5201 Lodge Rd., College Corner
huestonwoodslodge.com

Maumee Bay State Park
1750 State Park Rd., #2, Oregon
maumeebaylodge.com

Mohican State Park Lodge
1098 Ashland Co. Rd. 3006, Perrysville
mohicanlodge.com

Punderson State Park Lodge
11755 Kinsman Rd., Newbury
pundersonmanor.com

Salt Fork State Park Lodge
14755 Cadiz Rd., Lore City
saltforkparklodge.com

Shawnee State Park Lodge
4404B State Rte. 125, West Portsmouth
shawneeparklodge.com

The Lodge at Geneva-on-the-Lake
Ohio State Parks do not run the Lodge at Geneva-on-the-Lake, but
its close proximity to the state park puts it here on the list.
4888 N Broadway/State Rte. 534, Geneva-on-the-Lake
thelodgeatgeneva.com

HOP ABOARD A DINNER TRAIN
FOR AN EVENING OF ELEGANCE

The Cincinnati Dinner Train is a swinging good time with a 1940s vibe that takes you on a journey through southwestern Ohio. The train itself is a beautifully restored vintage locomotive, complete with elegant dining cars. The dinner served on board the Cincinnati Dinner Train is nothing short of exceptional. The chefs use only the freshest and highest-quality ingredients to prepare a delectable four-course meal that will delight your taste buds. From appetizers to entrées, every dish is expertly crafted and beautifully presented. Of course, the real star of the show is the experience itself. As you dine and relax on the train, big-band music fills the car, and you'll feel transported back in time to a bygone era of luxury and sophistication. The attentive and friendly staff will do everything they can to ensure your comfort and enjoyment, from refilling your wineglass to answering any questions about the train's history and the area it travels through. So why not climb aboard and see where the tracks take you?

2172 E Seymour Ave., Cincinnati, 513-791-7245
cincinnatidinnertrain.com

TIP
Book well in advance for this one-of-a-kind experience, or you may not snag a ticket to leave the station.

WATCH BIRDS
ON A WORLD-CLASS BOARDWALK

Bird-watchers from all corners of the world flock to Magee Marsh Wildlife Area in Ottawa County. This marsh is a popular destination that attracts more than 90,000 visitors with their binoculars and cameras during the "Biggest Birding Week in North America." The reason for this is the abundance of warblers that migrate through the area every year. You can witness these beautiful birds filling the brush and trees on their journey north to their summer homes. Walking on the boardwalk during this time is truly a magical experience that is impossible to describe in words. To add to the allure, the Magee Marsh Visitor Center has recently undergone a renovation that allows visitors to fully immerse themselves in the life of the animals and birds that call Magee Marsh their home. Whether you are an experienced bird-watcher or a novice, make sure to add Magee Marsh to your Ohio birding list.

13229 State Rte. 2, Oak Harbor
ohiodnr.gov/go-and-do/plan-a-visit/find-a-property/magee-marsh-wildlife-area

TIP
Magee Marsh Wildlife Refuge Boardwalk is wheelchair accessible and is a pack-in and pack-out destination.

OTHER GREAT OUTDOOR BIRDING DESTINATIONS NEARBY

East Harbor State Park
1169 N Buck Rd., Lakeside-Marblehead
ohiodnr.gov/go-and-do/plan-a-visit/find-a-property/
east-harbor-state-park

Maumee Bay State Park
1400 State Park Rd., Oregon
ohiodnr.gov/go-and-do/plan-a-visit/find-a-property/
maumee-bay-state-park

Howard Marsh Metropark
611 S Howard Rd., Curtice
metroparkstoledo.com/explore-your-parks/
howard-marsh-metropark

Metzger Marsh Wildlife Area, Curtice
ohiodnr.gov/go-and-do/plan-a-visit/find-a-property/
metzger-marsh-wildlife-area

Ottawa National Wildlife Refuge
14000 W State Rte. 2, Oak Harbor
fws.gov/refuge/ottawa

EMBARK ON
A MAJESTIC JOURNEY
INTO OHIO'S ONLY NATIONAL PARK

Did you know that the Cuyahoga River was once on fire? It's hard to believe, but it's true! The river caught fire, leading environmentalists to take action and create Cuyahoga Valley National Park. Today, the park boasts 33,000 acres of dense forests, lively wetlands, and rushing waterfalls, providing a natural habitat for beavers, deer, and native birds. Take a hike or bike along the Ohio & Erie Canal Towpath Trail, visit the historic visitors center, or paddle the river to experience the beauty of the park. Keep an ear out for the steam whistle, which blows at certain times of the year when the steam train returns to fill the valley with smoke. Any time of the year, you can ride the diesel trail. Whether you're planning a day trip or a weekend getaway, Cuyahoga Valley National Park has something for everyone, from outdoor recreation to history and culture.

Cuyahoga Valley National Park
6947 Riverview Rd., Peninsula, 440-717-3890
nps.gov/cuva

Cuyahoga Valley Scenic Railroad
330-439-5708
cvsr.org

CHEER
FOR THE OHIO STATE BUCKEYES

Ohio is a state that is genuinely passionate about its sports teams, especially the Ohio State Buckeyes football team. For nearly a century, fans have been flocking to Ohio Stadium, affectionately nicknamed "The Horseshoe," to support their home team and witness unforgettable moments in football history. Visitors to the stadium can not only catch legendary games but also take a tour of the impressive architecture, walk the same paths as iconic coach Woody Hayes, and soak up the immense scale of it all from the sidelines. With eyes closed, one can imagine the sound of "Hang On Sloopy" can be heard emanating from the Ohio State University Marching Band, renowned as the "best damn band in the land." Ohio State Buckeyes football is a true institution, and Ohio Stadium perfectly embodies the passion and dedication of the fans and players alike.

Ohio Stadium
411 Woody Hayes Dr., Columbus
ohiostatebuckeyes.com

DISCOVER LAKESIDE CHAUTAUQUA
TO RELAX AND REJUVENATE

As soon as you step through the gates of Lakeside Chautauqua, you'll feel like you've been transported to a magical place where your worries simply melt away. This charming resort town is filled with quaint cottages and a grand historic hotel overlooking the beautiful lake. It's a place where people come to slow down and savor the simple pleasures of life. Take a stroll through the town center where you can browse the shelves at Marilyn's or the Fine Print bookstore, indulge in a Toft's ice cream cone, and treat yourself to the famous fresh doughnuts from The Patio Restaurant's side window. To get around town easily, rent a golf cart or bike from Sypherd Cycles, a trusted local business serving the community for over 60 years. Take some time to focus on your wellness by playing pickleball in one of the greenspaces, or simply sit and soak in the breathtaking sunset while listening to the soft chime of the church bells. Lakeside Chautauqua is an extraordinary place that will leave a lasting impression on your soul.

Lakeside Chautauqua
236 Walnut Ave., Lakeside, 419-798-4461
lakesideohio.com

Marilyn's
223 Walnut Ave., Lakeside Marblehead, 419-798-5904

The Fine Print
202 Walnut Ave., Lakeside Marblehead, 419-702-7064
facebook.com/thefineprintlksd

The Patio Restaurant
182 Walnut Ave., Lakeside Marblehead, 419-798-9144
patiolakeside.com

Sypherd Cycles
182 Sycamore Ave., Lakeside Marblehead, 419-798-4124
sypherdcycles.com

MOSEY ALONG
ON THE BACK OF A HORSE

Marmon Valley Farm is a charming and family-friendly farm in Zanesfield. Spread across acres of serene countryside, this farm offers a wide range of activities and experiences for visitors of all ages. The farm is known for horseback riding and the variety of trails, visitors can saddle up and explore the beautiful surroundings while guided by experienced staff, experiences from scenic trail rides to pony rides for younger children. Marmon Valley Farm offers a host of other activities, like hayrides, nature hikes, and a stocked fishing pond. The farm also has a petting zoo, where children can interact with and learn about various farm animals.

But Marmon Valley Farm isn't just about fun—it's about learning, too. Educational programs, field trips, and summer camps teach children about farm life, animal care, and outdoor activities.

7754 State Rte. 292 S, Zanesfield
marmonvalley.com

TIP

Two weekends out of the year, Marmon Valley Farm offers "A Country Christmas," a unique hayride tour that brings you into the story of our Savior's birth; this event is memorable, heartwarming, and a must over the holiday season.

WALK A SKY BRIDGE
AND ZIP THROUGH THE SKY

USA Today calls ZipZone Outdoor Adventures "the #1 Adventure Park in Ohio"; it is a thrilling destination in Columbus, offering a perfect outdoor experience for adrenaline seekers. The park provides a variety of zip-lining courses that range from easy to challenging, but most of all, there is one that suits every adventure lover. One of the park's highlights is the Canopy Tour, which takes you through the treetops on a series of zip lines and sky bridges. This course offers stunning views of the surrounding forest and is perfect for those looking for a bit of adventure. This is a challenging course, and it will take effort! The Night Flight Tour is a must-try for those seeking a more adrenaline-fueled high-flying encounter. ZipZone Adventure Park also offers a Kids Park designed for young adventurers ages 4–7. This course features a variety of low zip lines and obstacles that are perfect for younger children, so everyone is involved in the high rope excursion!

7925 N High St., Columbus, 614-847-9477
zipzonetours.com

TIP

The philosophy of environmental protection and conservation is at the heart of the owners Lori and Jerrod Pingle's environmentally friendly building techniques for the course construction.

RACE DOWN
A TOBOGGAN SHOOT

Inside the Cleveland Metropark's Mill Stream Run Reservation in Strongsville lies the Chalet—home to the state's tallest and fastest toboggan chutes. As the winter season descends upon the area, the thrill seekers come out in droves, eager to experience the exhilarating rush of the twin toboggan runs. Climbing up the flights of wooden steps to the top, anticipation builds as each person eagerly awaits their turn. Once on the sled, the riders are sent hurtling down a 70-foot vertical drop on a solid sheet of ice, reaching speeds of up to 50 miles per hour. The sounds of unbridled joy echo throughout the park as each person races to the bottom. After the ride, visitors can warm up in the Chalet by the fire or indulge in a steaming mug of hot chocolate. Don't forget to explore the park, as Cleveland Metroparks offer year-round activities such as hiking, cycling, boating, backcountry hiking, and the chance to witness stunning waterfalls in all their natural beauty.

16200 Valley Pkwy., Strongsville, 440-572-9990
clevelandmetroparks.com

TIP
Book a timed ticket before you go to ensure you have a spot to ride.

PLAY BALL!
EMBRACE AMERICA'S FAVORITE PASTIME

Home to the Cincinnati Reds and the Cleveland Guardians, the Buckeye State is a place to come at least once in your lifetime to watch a baseball game at one of the iconic baseball fields. As a baseball fan, you might want to know more about the Cincinnati Reds, one of the oldest professional baseball teams in the country. The Reds were founded in 1881 and have won five World Series championships in their history. They play their home games at the Great American Ball Park, which is located in downtown Cincinnati right along the mighty Ohio River. The Cleveland Guardians were previously known as the Cleveland Indians until changing their name in 2021. The team was founded in 1901 and has won two World Series championships in its history. Plan your trip during one of their rivalry games to make your night of baseball even more memorable.

Cincinnati Reds
100 Joe Nuxhall Way, Cincinnati
mlb.com/reds

Cleveland Guardians
2401 Ontario St., Cleveland
mlb.com/guardians

FOLLOW THE BLUE BLAZES
FOR A 1,444-MILE HIKE AROUND OHIO

The Buckeye Trail is a 1,444-mile hiking trail that circles the state of Ohio, passing through some of the state's most beautiful natural areas. The trail is divided into 26 different sections, each with its own unique features and challenges. Hikers can expect to encounter a variety of terrain along the way, including forests, farmland, and rolling hills. The Buckeye Trail is open year-round and is accessible to hikers of all skill levels. Outdoor lovers will be able to experience Hocking Hills State Park and areas of Cuyahoga Valley National Park along this trail. Take time to visit historic stops along the way or grab a bite at an iconic restaurant in small towns. Whether you're an experienced hiker or just looking to explore Ohio's natural beauty, you'll be taken with the stunning scenery, rich history, and diverse terrain; it's no wonder that the Buckeye Trail has become a favorite of hikers from all over the country.

buckeyetrail.org

TIP
You don't have to do the whole trail simultaneously; many hikers do sections or out-and-back day trips.

CAMP AT A QUARRY
AT NATURAL SPRINGS RESORT

There are beautiful camping destinations throughout Ohio, but Natural Springs Resort in New Paris is one for your camping list. The resort boasts a 12-acre natural-fed spring lake that is so clear you can see all the way to the bottom, and the large sandy beach is perfect for swimming and playing on the Wibit, an inflatable jungle gym that's tons of fun for the whole family. But that's not all—scuba divers from all over come to Natural Springs Resort to practice open diving or even get certified. Ways to stay are numerous: you can book a fully stocked cabin, rent an RV, or bring your own; tent campers are welcome too! With so much to see and do, Natural Springs Resort is the ultimate RV destination for anyone looking to experience s'mores by the campfire while enjoying all the fun and excitement of a mini beach vacation.

500 S Washington St., New Paris, 937-437-5771
naturalspringsresort.com

Eddie's Grill in Geneva-on-the-Lake, Ohio

Groovy Plants Ranch in Marengo, Ohio

Clifton Mill Restaurant in Clifton, Ohio

Kayaking Ohio's waterways

National Museum of the United States Air Force
near Dayton, Ohio

Hocking Hills State Park Lodge in Logan, Ohio

G&R Tavern in Waldo, Ohio

Stockport Mill Inn and Restaurant in Stockport, Ohio

America's Packard Museum in Dayton, Ohio

ZipZone Outdoor Adventures in Columbus, Ohio

Columbus Zoo and Aquarium in Powell, Ohio

Marblehead Lighthouse in Marblehead, Ohio

Magee Marsh Visitor Center in Oak Harbor, Ohio

Float Troy in Troy, Ohio

The Avalon Theatre in Marysville, Ohio

Ludus
LKRSXB4H6R0EJ2KK

The Avalon Theatre
PRESENTS

Evening w Stella K. Cole

MON DEC 4, 2023 7:00 PM

THE AVALON THEATRE
121 SOUTH MAIN STREET, MARYSVILLE, OH, USA

GENERAL ADMISSION
GENERAL ADMISSION ($20)

SEAT: H2

Brandy Gleason

SEAT:

Brandy

ADMIT ONE

LKRSXB4H6R0EJ2KK

PADDLE DOWN
THE GREAT MIAMI RIVER

Anyone who loves the great outdoors should go kayaking on the Great Miami River. Adventures on the Great Miami River offer a range of paddling experiences, from serene stretches that are perfect for beginners to waters exciting enough for experienced kayakers, there is something here for everyone. As you paddle along the river, you'll be treated to stunning views of Ohio's natural beauty, including the wooded river banks and slightly rolling hills that make up the state's landscape. And, of course, the Great Miami River is also home to a diverse array of wildlife, including birds, fish, and turtles, making it an ideal excursion for nature lovers. Keep a keen eye out for white-tailed deer along your paddle. No matter what kind of kayaking experience you're looking for, you will find it here on the Great Miami River.

TIP
If you own your kayak, they offer a shuttle service for your paddle downriver.

Adventures on the Great Miami
1995 Ross Rd., Tipp City, 937-266-6252
greatmiami.net

Trapper John's
7141 London-Groveport Rd., Grove City, 614-877-4321
trapperjohnscanoeing.com

Hocking Hills Canoe Livery
12789 State Rte. 664, Logan, 740-216-4540
hockingriver.com

Mahoning River Adventures
75 N Leavitt Rd. NW, Leavittsburg, 330-967-0003
paddletheriver.com/mra

Morgan's Canoe Livery
513-932-7658
morganscanoe.com/ft-ancient

SEARCH
FOR BEACH GLASS
ON THE SHORES OF LAKE ERIE

If you're searching for an exciting and unusual outdoor activity in Ashtabula County, consider beachcombing at either Walnut Beach or Breakwater Beach. These beaches are well known for their plethora of beach glass, which can be discovered in a variety of colors and sizes along the shoreline. Beach glass is smooth, frosted, beautiful pieces of glass that are found on the beaches of the great lakes. They are formed from disgarded man-made glass products and are polished and refined by the waves and currents of lake waters. To increase your chances of finding some treasure, it's best to head out early in the morning before other beachcombers arrive. Whether you're an enthusiastic collector or simply seeking a fun way to spend a day in the sunshine, beach glass hunting at one of these beaches is an excellent opportunity to enjoy the natural beauty of Ohio's Lake Erie coastline.

TIP

Don't forget to pack your bucket and sunscreen; look among the small stones and pebbles for the glass; bring a spade to dig through the rocks to get the glass to the top.

Walnut Beach
Walnut Blvd. and Lake Ave., Ashtabula, 440-993-7036

Breakwater Beach at Geneva State Park
4499 Padanarum Rd., Geneva, 440-466-8400

OTHER BEACHES ALONG LAKE ERIE THAT ARE KNOWN FOR BEACH GLASS

Conneaut Township Park
480 Lake Rd., Conneaut, 440-599-7071
conneauttownshippark.com

Main Street Beach
Main St., Vermilion, 440-204-2490

TUCK INTO THE WOODS
FOR A CABIN STAY

Escape to a cozy cabin tucked away in the serene Hocking Hills region for a rejuvenating getaway. Liberty Log Lodging offers cabins that can comfortably accommodate groups ranging from two to 26, catering to every type of traveler. The cabins feature fully stocked kitchens and linens, ensuring a hassle-free stay with all the amenities of home. Spend your evenings by the firepit sharing stories or indulging in a relaxing soak in the hot tub while marveling at the unobstructed view of the starry night sky, which is one of the darkest in Ohio. While in the region, don't forget to visit the Old Man's Cave and the Hocking Hills State Park Visitor Center and explore the breathtaking waterfalls along the trails during your stay, or rent a pontoon boat at the Lake Logan Marina. You'll create unforgettable memories amid the tranquil beauty of nature no matter which cabin you choose.

Liberty Log Lodging
libertyloglodging.com

Hocking Hills State Park Visitor Center
19988 State Rte. 664, Logan, 740-385-6842

CLIMB ROCKS
AND SOAK IN NATURE

Experience an action-packed day of outdoor adventure with High Rock Adventures! Get ready to strap on your helmet and grab your rappelling gear as you explore the rocky terrain and gorgeous woods. Whether you're a thrill seeker looking for an adrenaline rush or a nature lover seeking a peaceful escape, High Rock Adventures has something for everyone. You can choose to go on the rappelling tour with exhilarating 70-foot drops that will get your heart racing or take a meditative guided hike through the private property and discover the medicinal plants along the naturescape. The best part is that High Rock Adventures can cater to all skill levels, so you don't have to worry about being left behind. Once you've had your fill of adventure in the great outdoors, stick around for the High Rock Escapes escape room challenge and see if you can solve all the riddles. And if that isn't enough, check out their rock shop featuring exquisitely polished stones or sensory stones!

High Rock Adventures
10108 Opossum Hollow Rd., Rockbridge, 740-385-9886
highrockadventures.com

High Rock Escapes
740-385-9886
highrockescapes.com

DRIVE
ONE OF OHIO'S SCENIC BYWAYS

Ohio's 27 scenic byways are a must-see for anyone who loves the great outdoors, beautiful scenery, and the open road. With over 2,000 miles of scenic byways, Ohio offers some of the most picturesque drives in the United States. From rolling hills to rugged coastlines, Ohio's scenic byways offer something for every road tripper. The Buckeye State's scenic byways are perfect for a leisurely drive, with plenty of opportunities to stop and take in the views. One of Ohio's most famous scenic byways is the Hocking Hills Scenic Byway. This 26-mile stretch of road takes visitors through the stunning Hocking Hills region, which features ancient rock formations, cascading waterfalls, and spectacular vistas. The byway offers plenty of opportunities for hiking, biking, and wildlife watching, making it a perfect destination for outdoor enthusiasts. Another must-see scenic byway in Ohio is the Lake Erie Coastal Ohio Trail. This 293-mile route takes visitors along Lake Erie's scenic coastline, with plenty of opportunities to stop and explore charming towns and villages, like Vermillion and Conneaut, along the way. Whether you're a nature lover or simply enjoy a good road trip, Ohio's scenic byways are not to be missed.

transportation.ohio.gov/traveling/ohio-byways

UNCOVER
THE MAGIC OF WINTER
AT SNOW TRAILS SKI RESORT
IN MANSFIELD

As winter approaches, the anticipation for the opening of Snow Trails ski resort in the Buckeye State builds with each passing day. As soon as the announcement is made, eager skiers and snowboarders flock to the resort to experience the magic of the winter wonderland. Stepping into the complex, the bustling energy of the snow-covered slopes is palpable as skiers and snowboarders make their way to the Snow Trails Lodge. The lodge boasts a restaurant, cafeteria, two full bars, and a spacious deck that offers a breathtaking view of the slopes. With activities for all skill levels from beginner to expert, Snow Trails has opportunities for all winter fun seekers. Glow tubing on a crisp winter night or during the day is another way to get out and enjoy the Ohio ski slopes. Whiz your way down the tubing hill as the wind whips by; it's euphoric!

3100 Possum Run Rd., Mansfield, 419-774-9818
snowtrails.com

TIP
Always check snow conditions before going; Ohio tends to have bipolar weather.

MARVEL
AT THE RE-CREATED INDUSTRIAL PARK

If you're looking for a serene and strikingly beautiful escape in Ohio, look no further than Ariel-Foundation Park. This stunning 250-acre public park in Mount Vernon boasts an impressive range of green spaces, including three restored quarry lakes, wetlands, and forested areas. Spend an afternoon fishing or kayaking in the lakes, or stop by the River of Glass, a beautiful art installation that pays homage to the PPG Glass Factory. With trails winding throughout the park, it's easy to explore on foot, bike, or even roller skates. And don't miss the Rastin Observation Tower, a 60-foot-tall structure that offers breathtaking views of the park and surrounding countryside. Just be prepared to climb the spiral staircase to reach the top! For a perfect escape, grab a picnic lunch at North Main Café in Mount Vernon, book a room at Mount Vernon Grand on the square, and visit the unique cast-iron dog fountain.

Ariel-Foundation Park
10 Pittsburgh Ave., Mount Vernon
740-501-9293
arielfoundationpark.org

Mount Vernon Grand
12 Public Sq., Mount Vernon
844-700-1717
mountvernongrand.com

North Main Café
108 N Main St., Mount Vernon
740-326-6574
north-main-cafe.com

Dog Fountain
201 S Main St., Mount Vernon

GET DIRTY
AT THE RACETRACK

You can't miss the sound of the roaring engines when you park your car at Eldora Speedway in New Weston affectionately referred to as The Big E™. This dirt track is a popular destination for racing enthusiasts from all over the region. With its high-speed track and down-to-earth facilities, it's no wonder why so many people flock to this venue every year. The speedway boasts a half-mile dirt track that is perfect for quick racing. Fans can expect to see a wide variety of racing events, including sprint cars, modifieds, late models, and more. The track is known for its fast speeds and high banked turns, providing a thrilling experience for both drivers and spectators alike. Sit up high in the bleachers to avoid eating all the dirt that can get thrown up as the cars speed past.

13929 State Rd. 118, New Weston, 937-338-3815
eldoraspeedway.com

TIP
Buy the pit pass and get up close with the drivers to see their cars and get to know the teams.

Airstream Heritage Center in Jackson Center, Ohio

CULTURE
AND HISTORY

TURN ON THE LIGHTS
AND THANK THOMAS EDISON

Did you know that one of the greatest inventors in American history was born in Milan, Ohio, in 1847? His name was Thomas Alva Edison, and he was born in a small but beautiful brick home in the middle of winter. Milan was a busy port town near Lake Erie, and Edison's father chose to settle there because of the trading opportunities and the potential for his growing family. If you want to learn more about Edison's early childhood, you should check out the home and museum tours at the Thomas Edison Birthplace Museum. You'll discover that Edison was an ornery kid who was eventually homeschooled because of his behavior. You'll also get to see some of his inventions up close, listen to an Edison Phonograph with wax cylinders, and learn about his short-lived involvement in moving pictures. Keep in mind that the museum's hours vary by season, so be sure to check before you go. As Thomas Edison once said, "I have not failed. I've just found 10,000 ways that won't work."

9 N Edison Dr., Milan, 419-499-2135
tomedison.org

TIP

Visit the town of Milan and see the picturesque town square to shop at D'Vine Design and The Baker on the Square. If time allows, explore the Milan Museum, which takes up a historic block.

D'Vine Design
29 Park St., Milan, 419-499-8463

The Baker on the Square
47 Front St. Public Sq., Milan, 567-401-6120
bakeronthesquare.com

The Milan Museum
10 Edison Dr., Milan, 419-499-2968
milanhistory.org

SOAR THROUGH
AMERICA'S AIR FORCE HISTORY

The National Museum of the United States Air Force is truly a bucket list of bucket-list destinations for anyone interested in military aviation. With its impressive collection of 360-plus aerospace artifacts and missiles, it offers a unique opportunity to experience history through the eyes of a pilot. The museum is divided into four connected buildings, allowing guests to easily navigate through the different exhibits and galleries. One of the highlights of the museum is the Doolittle Raiders goblets, which pay tribute to the brave pilots who carried out the famous raid on Tokyo in 1942. Additionally, the memorial park is a beautiful and moving tribute to the men and women who have served in the US Air Force. Visitors will also have the chance to see *Air Force One* up close, as well as the legendary *Memphis Belle* and "Hanoi Taxi." For an even more immersive experience, the museum offers hands-on exhibits, simulators, and IMAX movies. Plan to spend plenty of time exploring this incredible museum—you won't regret it!

1100 Spaatz St., Wright-Patterson AFB (near Dayton), 937-255-3286
nationalmuseum.af.mil

TIP
Be aware of the screening process upon entrance to the museum and check hours in advance; they are subject to change.

NAVIGATE THE EVOLUTION
OF OHIO'S PACKARD HISTORY

If you're planning a trip to Ohio and love classic cars, visit two Packard museums while exploring the Buckeye State. Packard automobiles were known for their unique European style with American durability, and after World War II, they began to evolve into family cars with advertising campaigns targeting working-class families. Both museums are packed full of original and fully restored Packards, each unique. America's Packard Museum is fascinating as it's the only restored Packard dealership that operates as a museum. Visitors find themselves fully involved as they walk among these treasures, and Maude Gamble Nippert's car stands out with a story all its own. Don't miss Al Capone's car, delivered with used casings in the back seat. The National Packard Museum in Northeast Ohio is another excellent museum that invites visitors to learn all there is to know about Packard and the companies they operated. Two notable cars on display are the rare early 1950s Packard Pan Americans; they are stunners. Plan your visit carefully to ensure you have enough time to explore these fantastic museums.

National Packard Museum
1899 Mahoning Ave. NW, Warren, 330-394-1899
packardmuseum.org

America's Packard Museum
420 S Ludlow St., Dayton, 937-226-1710
americaspackardmuseum.org

EXPERIENCE VIBRANT WONDERS
IN OHIO'S MOST COLORFUL CAVERNS

Ohio Caverns is the place to be for those seeking an unforgettable underground adventure. The caverns offer tours that take you deep into the subterranean world, where you can explore this unique environment's stunning sights and sounds. The sound of water greets visitors as they descend 44 or 38 steps, depending on the tour chosen. Initially explored in 1897, these privately owned caverns have become a popular destination for rockhounds and adventure seekers alike. Be prepared for the tight twists and turns on the tour as each reveals something new. One of the tour's highlights is the Crystal King, Ohio's largest stalactite—you'll definitely want to snap a photo of this natural wonder. Ohio Caverns is open year-round, and each tour lasts about an hour. The temperature in the caverns remains a comfortable 52 degrees all day, every day, so dress accordingly. If you have limited mobility, be sure to inquire about the reservation-only tour.

2210 E State Rte. 245, West Liberty, 937-465-4017
ohiocaverns.com

TIP

Grab an Ohio Cave Trail Guide and get a stamp, then visit all the stops: Perry's Cave, Seneca Caverns, and Crystal Cave.

Perry's Cave Family Fun Center
979 Catawba Ave., Put-in-Bay, 419-285-2283
perryscave.com

Seneca Caverns
15248 E Township Rd. 178, Bellevue, 419-483-6711
senecacavernsohio.com

Crystal Cave
978 Catawba Ave., Put-In-Bay, 419-285-2811
heinemanswinery.com/crystalcave.asp

TRACE THE PATH
TO WHERE AVIATION BEGAN

Dayton, also known as the Gem City, is a truly unique destination that captures the essence of American history and innovation. It is where the Wright brothers famously invented the airplane, and NCR built cash registers. The city is home to Carillon Historical Park, a museum showcasing the rich history of Dayton and the United States. Visitors of all ages can engage with interactive exhibits and explore re-created and moved buildings that offer a glimpse into the past. The park also includes a roundhouse filled with trains, the Wright Brothers National Museum, and a facility dedicated to the Great Flood of 1913. Inside the main museum, visitors can marvel at a beautifully restored wooden carousel and browse the gift shop for souvenirs. After a day of exploring, be sure to stop by the Carillon Brewing Company, the nation's only brewery set in a museum, where you can taste spirits made using traditional methods.

1000 Carillon Blvd., Dayton
daytonhistory.org

TIP

While at Carillon Historical Park, plan to visit all the aviation sites in Dayton. Let your love of history fly.

Wright Brothers Memorial
2380 Memorial Rd., Wright-Patterson Air Force Base

Huffman Prairie Flying Field Interpretive Center
2380 Memorial Rd., Wright-Patterson Air Force Base

Dayton Air Show at Dayton International Airport
3700 Wright Dr., Vandalia
daytonairshow.com

Woodland Cemetery
118 Woodland Ave., Dayton
woodlandcemetery.org/landmark-maps

Dayton Aviation Heritage National Historical Park
Wright-Dunbar Interpretive Center, 16 S Williams St., Dayton
nps.gov/daav/index.htm

Paul Laurence Dunbar House Historic Site
219 N Paul Laurence Dunbar St., Dayton
nps.gov/places/dunbar-house.htm

Hawthorn Hill Mansion
1000 Carillon Blvd., Dayton
daytonhistory.org/visit/dayton-history-sites/hawthorn-hill

WALK IN THE FOOTSTEPS
OF EARLY AMERICAN SOLDIERS

Ohio has a rich history as the gateway to the West, with early pioneers braving the unknown to seek out new opportunities and fresh starts. Along the way, these pioneers encountered many challenges, including skirmishes with other nations and Native Americans who had lived in the area for generations. Despite the passing of time, Ohio has done an excellent job of preserving and reconstructing the forts that remain from this era. Today, visitors can learn about the lives of early American soldiers and what day-to-day life was like on the frontier by visiting Historic Fort Steubenville, which was constructed in 1786 and still stands today. Fort Recovery is another important site in Ohio's history, as it was the location where Chief Little Turtle of the Miami defeated St. Claire, resulting in over 900 American soldier deaths—the worst defeat of the American army on American soil. Fort Laurens, Ohio's only Revolutionary War fort, was built in 1778 as a wilderness outpost, while Fort Meigs was constructed during the War of 1812 to protect against British attack. General William Henry Harrison once said, "When the impartial historian records his preservation of Fort Meigs, the reader will find a monument which no time can decay."

TIP

Each fort has differing seasons and hours;
check the websites before planning your trip.

Fort Laurens
11067 Fort Laurens Rd. NW, Bolivar
ohiohistory.org/visit/browse-historical-sites/fort-laurens

Fort Meigs
29100 W River Rd., Perrysburg
fortmeigs.org

Fort Recovery State Museum
1 Fort Site St., Fort Recovery
fortrecoverymuseum.com

Historic Fort Steuben
120 S 3rd St., Steubenville
oldfortsteuben.com

DELVE INTO
PRESIDENTIAL HISTORY

Ohio's storied past boasts a remarkable distinction: it serves as the birthplace of eight US presidents. This honor is one that the state holds in high regard and takes great pride in. Visitors to Ohio can embark on an unforgettable journey, spending weeks exploring the well-preserved historical sites, grand homes, expansive libraries, revered memorials, and honored gravesites of these presidents. From the shores of Lake Erie to the charming town of Cincinnati nestled along the Ohio River, these sites are spread throughout the state, making it essential to plan your journey carefully to ensure that you have enough time to visit them all. Immerse yourself in the rich history of Ohio and discover the stories that have shaped America's past.

TIP
Research each area because many historical stops are connected to the central location.

William Howard Taft National Historic Site
2038 Auburn Ave., Cincinnati, 513-684-3262
nps.gov/wiho/index.htm

U. S. Grant Birthplace
1551 Ohio 232, Moscow, 513-497-0492
ohiohistory.org/visit/browse-historical-sites/
u-s-grant-birthplace

Warren G. Harding Presidential Sites
380 Mt. Vernon Ave., Marion, 800-600-6894
hardingpresidentialsites.org

Rutherford B. Hayes Presidential Library & Museums
Spiegel Grove, Fremont, 419-332-2081
rbhayes.org

James A. Garfield National Historic Site
8095 Mentor Ave., Mentor, 440-255-8722
nps.gov/jaga/index.htm

McKinley Presidential Library & Museum
800 McKinley Monument Dr. NW, Canton, 330-455-7043
mckinleymuseum.org

William Henry Harrison Tomb
41 Cliff Rd., North Bend, 844-288-7709
ohiohistory.org/visit/browse-historical-sites/
william-henry-harrison-tomb

COMMEMORATE AMERICA'S FIRST LADIES
AT THE FIRST LADIES
NATIONAL HISTORIC SITE

While American history is full of destinations celebrating our presidents, it's essential not to overlook the women who stood by their sides, hosted important dignitaries, and ran the White House. The First Ladies National Historic Site in Canton is dedicated to honoring these remarkable women and their contributions to our nation. Take a tour of the Education Center, where rotating exhibits provide a fascinating glimpse into the elegant lifestyles of these iconic women. If you're interested in exploring further, purchase tickets in advance for the Saxon House, where you can walk through the childhood home of Ida McKinley. This stunningly restored Victorian home, furnished with original pieces from the McKinley family, provides a unique window into the past and is not to be missed.

205 Market Ave. S, Canton, 330-452-0876
nps.gov/fila

TIP
Free parking is located beside the Saxon House.

SAIL THROUGH
THE NATIONAL MUSEUM
OF THE GREAT LAKES

Have you heard of the National Museum of the Great Lakes in Toledo? This remarkable museum is dedicated to preserving and sharing the history of the Great Lakes. Founded in 1983 as the Great Lakes Historical Society and renamed the National Museum of the Great Lakes in 2006, the museum boasts hands-on exhibits that tell the stories of the people and events that have shaped the Great Lakes region. Take advantage of the opportunity to walk through the 617-foot iron ore freighter *Col. James M. Schoonmaker* and stand behind the wheel to experience what it is like to captain a large vessel. The Museum Tug *Ohio* is also a must-see exhibit for anyone interested in the history of shipping in the Lake region.

1701 Front St., Toledo, 419-214-5000
nmgl.org

TIP

The best time to visit is in April–October when all the exhibits are open; the outdoor displays are seasonal.

APPRECIATE THE NATIVE AMERICAN HISTORY
AT EARTHEN MOUNDS

The word *Ohio* takes its name from the Iroquois word *ohiːyo*, which means "the great river." Ohio's Native American heritage is rich and filled with deep-rooted traditions in early history, from hunter-gatherers to the Mound Builders whose earthen mounds still rise to meet the sun to this day. Throughout the state, museums, powwows, and earthworks commemorate, educate, and guard the ancient history of the Native American people. Earthworks are one of the most prominent remnants that can be explored and understood; however, there still remains a mystery about why some of these were constructed. Ohio is home to the world's largest effigy mound in Peebles, known as the Serpent Mound, representing a snake with a curved tail. The Hopewell Culture National Historical Park in Chillicothe is home to six archeological sites encapsulated in one national park; spend the day learning and stopping at each one.

TIP

Ohio's Native American sites are to be honored and respected; be mindful as you visit and learn.

Serpent Mound Historical Site
3850 State Rte. 73, Peebles, 800-752-2757
ohiohistory.org/visit/browse-historical-sites/serpent-mound

Fort Ancient Earthworks & Nature Preserve
6123 State Rte. 350, Oregonia, 513-932-4421
ohiohistory.org/visit/browse-historical-sites/
fort-ancient-earthworks-nature-preserve

Newark Earthworks
455 Hebron Rd., Heath, 740-344-0498
ohiohistory.org/visit/browse-historical-sites/
newark-earthworks

Sunwatch Indian Village
2301 W River Rd., Dayton, 937-268-8199
boonshoft.org/sunwatch-2

Hopewell Culture National Historical Park
16062 State Rte. 104, Chillicothe, 740-774-1125
nps.gov/hocu

WALK THROUGH
OHIO'S OLDEST SETTLEMENT

Marietta was founded by the Ohio Company in 1788 as the first permanent settlement in the Northwest Territory. History seeps from every corner of this historic town. Campus Martius is the gatekeeper of all this rich history where visitors can come to learn of Ohio's beginnings. Inside, you will find a National Historic Landmark, the Rufus Putnam House, built in 1788, the only surviving part of the original Campus Martius. Plan on coming when a guided tour of the Rufus Putnam house is scheduled; significant details of the corner block of the fort are pointed out, and you don't want to miss those. While most of the museum is dedicated to Ohio's history, there are many artifacts from the Ohio Company, the American Revolution, and the early days of the Northwest Territory.

Campus Martius
601 2nd St., Marietta, 740-373-3750
mariettamuseums.org

TIP

While enjoying historic Marietta, visit the *Memorial to the Start Westward of the United States* by Gutzon Borglum, sculptor of Mount Rushmore, and the Ohio River Museum.

State Westward Monument
300 Block Front St., Muskingum Park, Marietta
startwestward1787.com

Ohio River Museum
601 Front St., Marietta, 740-373-3750
mariettamuseums.org/ohio-river-museum

GO BEHIND BARS
IN SEARCH OF GHOSTLY GUESTS

The Ohio State Reformatory, also known as the Mansfield Reformatory, is a historic prison in Mansfield. This notorious facility was built between 1886 and 1910 and remained operational until its closure in 1990. This prison has been featured in several films, TV shows, and music videos. Still, it is most famous for being the primary filming location for the iconic movie *The Shawshank Redemption*. Visitors can indulge in all things Hollywood with the guided tour, which offers a peek into props and behind-the-scenes stories. For those who love the paranormal, there are adults-only hunts where investigators roam through cells and halls in search of ghostly guests. During Halloween, the prison transforms into a nightmarish maze as the Warden's Widow leads her maniacal inmates and deformed guards through the world's largest freestanding cell block, creating an eerie atmosphere bound to spook even the bravest of souls.

100 Reformatory Rd., Mansfield, 419-522-2644
mrps.org

TIP
If you have extra time, take the day and do the whole *Shawshank Redemption* driving tour.

DRIVE TO ONE OF THE ICONIC LIGHTHOUSES
OF OHIO

Ohio may not have a coastline on the ocean, but it does have a significant history with lighthouses and is home to several lighthouses that served as necessary navigational aids for sailors and fishermen in the 19th and early 20th centuries. Some of these lighthouses, like the Marblehead Lighthouse, are still standing today and have become popular tourist attractions. Marblehead lighthouse, the oldest lighthouse in continuous operation on the Great Lakes, is open to the public. Visitors can climb to the top for a breathtaking view of Lake Erie during the summertime, and the state park grounds are available year-round. Be sure to wear sturdy shoes for the trek up the 77 winding steps to the top of the lighthouse—it is not for the faint of heart. The Marblehead Lighthouse is one of the smallest Ohio state parks; it is a perfect spot for a picnic.

110 Lighthouse Dr., Marblehead
marbleheadlighthouseohio.org

ohiodnr.gov/go-and-do/plan-a-visit/find-a-property/
marblehead-lighthouse-state-park

WANDER THE HALLS
OF OHIO'S CASTLES

Wrapped among the dense forest lies a captivating castle that will transport you to the era of knights and fair maidens. Ravenwood Castle is a serene haven for modern-day respite seekers who yearn to disconnect from the hustle and bustle of daily life and immerse themselves in the lush, tranquil surroundings. The castle offers a range of accommodation options, from themed rooms within the castle walls to cozy cottages in the medieval village. Wander along the winding paths that meander through the woods and find solace in the serene gardens. However, if you're in the mood for something a bit more thrilling, join in on one of the weekend murder mysteries, where the guests themselves play the roles of the characters, and the murderer could be lurking among you. If board games are more your speed, you'll be delighted to know that Ravenwood Castle is home to an unparalleled community of gamers. While unplugging from the world, discover a new game to play from the main castle office.

65666 Bethel Rd., New Plymouth, 740-596-2606
ravenwoodcastle.com

TIP

Dining is available on the property; anything off-site is 15 minutes away or more.

OTHER CASTLES IN OHIO

Piatt Castle
10051 Township Rd. 47, West Liberty, 937-465-2821
piattcastle.org

GreatStone Castle
429 N Ohio Ave., Sidney, 937-498-4728
greatstonecastle.com

Landoll's Mohican Castle
Landoll's Mohican Castle is highlighted in
100 Things to Do in Ohio's Amish Country Before You Die.
561 Township Rd. 3352, Loudonville, 419-994-3427
landollsmohicancastle.com

Loveland Castle
12075 Shore Dr., Loveland, 513-683-4686 (for a recorded message)
lovelandcastle.com

Squire's Castle
3037 SOM Ctr. Rd., Willoughby Hills, 440-473-3370
clevelandmetroparks.com/parks/visit/parks/
north-chagrin-reservation/squire-s-castle

GO BACK IN TIME
TO LEARN OHIO'S HISTORY

The Ohio History Connections main campus in Columbus is dedicated to preserving the rich and fascinating history of the state with the Ohio History Center museum and the Ohio Village living history community. The Ohio History Center boasts a vast collection of precious artifacts and documents, making it an invaluable resource for anyone eager to delve deeper into Ohio's historical past. The museum is a true gem and might even take you by surprise, offering a range of exhibits that cover the state's prehistoric era, its contribution to the Civil War, and even a Lustron home, among others. Visitors also can make appointments to explore the extensive library and archives, which hold a wealth of information about Ohio's culture and heritage. Ohio Village is a particular favorite of history buffs, where dedicated interpreters stand ready throughout the village's buildings and town square to answer any questions. The main campus in Columbus also serves as a gateway for visitors to discover the 50-plus other locations throughout the state that the Ohio History Connection preserves, showing the depth and breadth of the organization's commitment to preserving the past.

The Ohio History Center
800 E 17th Ave., Columbus, 614-297-2300
ohiohistory.org/visit/ohio-history-center

GET A GLIMPSE OF ANNIE OAKLEY
AT THE GARST MUSEUM

Are you curious about the life and legacy of Annie Oakley? The Garst Museum offers a fascinating exhibit dedicated to this iconic figure. Despite the Hollywood portrayal of Oakley as a rough and wild cowgirl, the display highlights her softer, more feminine side. The exhibit is beautifully arranged and pays tribute to the legendary sharpshooter who was born in Darke County. Visitors can learn about Oakley's life and career and even see some of her personal items on display. If you're lucky, you may even get the opportunity to hold her 1910 J. Stevens .22 caliber deluxe target rifle with a Scheutzen but during special events. This is a truly epic and once-in-a-lifetime experience. The Garst Museum was established in 1902 by Annie and George Garst and is now located in a historic building in downtown Greenville, which was once the site of Fort Greene Ville, a critical frontier fort during the early 19th century. As you walk through the galleries, the Garst Museum will surprise you with its various exhibits, from the renowned journalist, author, and broadcaster Lowell Thomas to the Treaty of Greenville and the beginnings of Ohio.

205 N Broadway, Greenville, 937-548-5250
garstmuseum.org

SPEND THE WEEKEND
IN SAUDER VILLAGE

Take a weekend in the summer to explore one of Ohio's premier living history museums in Archbold, offering visitors an extraordinary and immersive experience of life in a 19th-century Ohio village. The village is comprised of more than 40 historic buildings, including homes, farms, and shops, where costumed interpreters demonstrate traditional crafts and trades such as blacksmithing, weaving, and woodworking. Enjoy a ride on the horse-drawn carriage, attend a school lesson in the one-room schoolhouse, or participate in hands-on activities such as candle making or butter churning. The village also features a working farm where visitors can interact with farm animals and learn about the daily life of a farm family. Hop on board the train in the re-created 1920s main street and then grab a hand-spun milkshake in the soda fountain. What is more, Sauder Village also offers modern amenities such as a full-service sit-down restaurant serving delicious food year-round, a village full of shopping, and beautiful overnight accommodations. With its welcoming old-time feel and interactive experiences, this historic stop should make your bucket list.

22611 State Rte. 2, Archbold, 800-590-9755
saudervillage.org

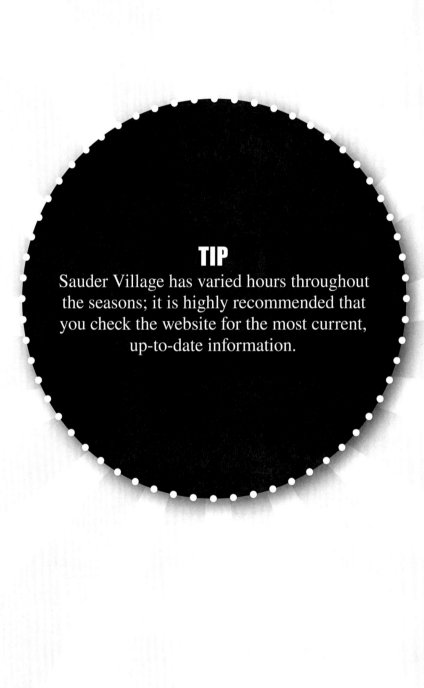

TIP
Sauder Village has varied hours throughout the seasons; it is highly recommended that you check the website for the most current, up-to-date information.

TOUR AMERICA'S MOST ICONIC ALUMINUM CAMPER
AT THE AIRSTREAM HERITAGE CENTER

You see the iconic silver bullet Airstreams being pulled down the interstate, and they are memorable. The classic Airstream travel trailers and touring coaches are made right here in Ohio. For over 100 years, Airstream has been making high-quality travel trailers, and in 2021, the Airstream Heritage Center opened to the public, bringing to life the rich cultural history. Learn about the caravans that have gone around the world, check out refurbished and original units, and imagine yourself traveling the country in one. While there, book a tour of the Airstream factory, where each Airstream is made to order by hand! Visit the Mothership, where memories and history are still being made, one rivet at a time.

"Don't live in the past or future . . . make history."—Airstream founder Wally Byam

1001 W Pike St., Jackson Center, 937-596-6849
airstream.com/heritage-center

WALK THE HISTORY
OF OHIO'S POOR FARMS

The Wood County Infirmary, later known as the Wood County Home, served the county's poor, elderly, and disabled starting in 1869. The site was transitioned into a nursing home in the 1920s but eventually closed in 1971. The remaining residents were moved to the newly constructed Wood County Nursing Home, now known as Wood Haven Health Care. The Wood County Historical Society dedicated the site as the Wood County Historical Center & Museum in 1976. Today, the Wood County Museum stands as the most complete infirmary site in Ohio. It has received multiple awards for its thematically rotating exhibits showcasing the history of the former infirmary farm, also known as a poor farm, and the people of Wood County.

In addition to the exhibits and historic buildings, the Wood County Museum hosts a range of educational programs, workshops, and events throughout the year. These events cater to both children and adults and provide opportunities to learn more about the history and culture of the region.

Wood County Home
13660 County Home Rd., Bowling Green, 419-352-0967
woodcountyhistory.org

UNWIND AND DINE
AT THE LAST STANDING MILL ON THE MUSKINGUM RIVER

Stockport, found in Morgan County, is like a journey back in time. The town's location near the Muskingum River adds to its charm and antiquity, reminding visitors of a past era. Founded in 1843, Stockport used to be a bustling hub of trade during the river's busy days. Today, the Stockport Mill Inn and Restaurant sits where the former grain and hydroelectric mill stood, offering guests an exceptional and unforgettable experience. The Stockport Mill was constructed in March 1906 by the Dover brothers. It immediately started elevating wheat and, by 1908, began providing electricity to the town. Nowadays, the mill produces its own electricity and is situated on dam #6 to maximize water pressure usage. The Stockport Mill Inn and Restaurant is an enchanting historic site located in the heart of the Ohio River Valley. Its picturesque setting on the dam provides guests with a calming dining experience, with stunning views of the river and the surrounding landscape. The restaurant is renowned for its outstanding cuisine, which features locally sourced components and traditional American dishes.

1995 Broadway Ave., Stockport, 740-559-2822
stockportmill.com

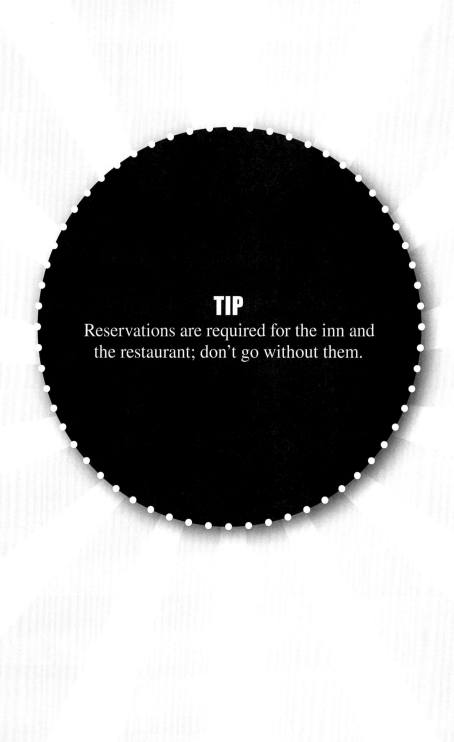

TIP

Reservations are required for the inn and the restaurant; don't go without them.

b.a. Sweetie Candy Company in Cleveland, Ohio

SHOPPING AND FASHION

WATCH JACK PINE BLOW GLASS
IN THE WOODS OF HOCKING HILLS

Every year, thousands flock to Jack Pine Studio for his glass pumpkin patch, where thousands of colorfully and artfully created handblown pieces are decorated and placed in the "pumpkin patch." Each year, I even go to buy a pumpkin to grace my fall Thanksgiving table. While coming to this event might be unique, it is busy, so plan a trip at any time of the year; trust me, it is worth the trip. The hot shop is open each day with craftspeople creating different kinds of glass creations, from Christmas ornaments to hanging suncatchers. If you love what you see, book one of the group or private sessions to design your very own personal glass-blown item. Jack Pine is a native of the southern Ohio area; his craftsmanship and artistry bring a deeper dimension and beauty to the Hocking Hills region.

21397 OH-180, Laurelville, 740-332-2223
jackpinestudio.com

TRAVEL BACK IN TIME
TO THE OLDEST OPERATING STORE IN OHIO

When you think of an old-time general store, you expect penny candy and hard-to-find items; the End of the Commons has all that and more. Since 1840, this historic building has been serving the community, and today, it stands as a testament to how good customer service with high-quality items keeps a business around. Over time, they have added many new things, with homemade Amish baked goods topping the list of why people keep coming back. Freshly made fry pies are a local and national favorite; these delectable treats are filled with tempting pie fillings, deep fried to a golden brown then drizzled with sweet icing. Clarksville Sweets is the newest edition, featuring over 40 handmade premium chocolates and over 30 gourmet popcorn flavors. Visitors can watch the candy and popcorn-making process through four large windows. Bringing kids? Feed the goats and chickens in the mini goat barn before you leave.

End of the Commons General Store
8719 State Rte. 534, Mesopotamia, 440-693-4295
endofthecommons.com

TASTE THE BEST OF CLEVELAND
AT THE WEST SIDE MARKET

The West Side Market is a vibrant and bustling stop in Cleveland. This historic market, dating back to 1912, is home to a diverse range of vendors and a rich cultural heritage. The main draw at the West Side Market is the wide array of fresh produce, meats, and seafood available. Wander through the aisles and marvel at the colorful selection of fruits and vegetables, or sample the deliciously aromatic spices and herbs. The market is also renowned for its high-quality meats, with butchers offering an impressive variety of cuts, from prime steaks to flavorful sausages. You'll also find a treasure trove of artisanal products and specialty goods. Browse through the stalls and discover unique cheeses, delectable pastries, homemade pasta, and a myriad of international delicacies. The West Side Market is not just about food and shopping; it is also a place to immerse yourself in the local culture and history. Take a guided tour to learn about the market's architectural significance and fascinating past. The iconic clock tower is a symbol of Cleveland and provides a picturesque backdrop for memorable photographs.

1979 W 25th St., Cleveland, 216-664-3387
westsidemarket.org

GET YOUR FLOWER POWER ON
AT GROOVY PLANTS RANCH

Plant shopping is at its finest at Groovy Plants Ranch in Marengo. What started out as a passion project for Jared Hughes at 18 has exploded into a gardening destination that people come to from all over the Midwest. What you will find at this over-the-top greenhouse is a variety of plants that will blow your mind. Houseplants, perennials, flowers, rare and unusual plants, and garden favorites are all displayed throughout the indoor and outdoor shopping spaces. Kids love this place, too, with an abandoned airplane, hobbit playhouse, planted VW Bug, and full-sized unicorn. Bring some of your plant-loving besties during one of their workshops to create something beautiful to take home; the classes are informative as well as entertaining. Food trucks are available on most weekends; check their online calendar for events.

4140 County Rd. 15, Marengo, 740-675-2681
groovyplantsranch.com

TIP
Plan your trip wisely; weekends and holidays are packed with plant lovers; for a more relaxed shopping trip, visit during the week.

SHOP THE WORLD
AT JUNGLE JIM'S
INTERNATIONAL MARKET

Jungle Jim's is Ohio's most unique grocery store, filled with more than 180,000 items from all over the world. Shoppers will be speechless as they enter the store for the first time, and they might even get a little lost, so grab a map before venturing too far in. Every square inch is filled with extraordinary items, so plan to be there for at least a couple of hours. Sections are labeled by country, making the experience a foodie's dream walk through the world, one that can't be replicated anywhere else! Every aisle will have you adding new things to your cart, from the hottest hot sauces and tempting root beers to a whole shark or alligator.

Surprises are around every corner, from Robin Hood hiding in the trees in England to a bathroom experience that will leave you smiling. One might even call it the theme park of grocery stores.

5440 Dixie Hwy., Fairfield
4450 Eastgate S Dr., Cincinnati, 513-674-6000
junglejims.com

TIP
Plan your visit around the International Craft Beer Festival or the Weekend of Fire.

SAVOR THE CHEESE
AT GRANDPA'S CHEESEBARN

Grandpa's Cheesebarn in Ashland is a cheese lover's dream come true. With its rich family history, starting with Grandpa Yarman, and a mouthwatering selection of cheeses, it has become a beloved landmark in the area. When you enter Grandpa's Cheesebarn, you are immediately greeted by the aroma of freshly made cheese and the sight of shelves filled with an impressive variety of artisanal cheeses and bulk foods. From classic cheddar to exotic combinations, there is something to satisfy every palate. Not sure you will like a flavor? No worries, they offer free samples! Grandpa's Cheesebarn is more than just a cheese store; it is a destination that celebrates the art of cheese making and the joy of indulging in high-quality products. Oh, but there is more; right next door is Sweeties Chocolates, where you can get homemade confections that will make your taste buds thank you.

668 US-HWY 250 E, Ashland, 419-281-3202
grandpascheesebarn.com

GET LOST
IN A BOOK

If you're a book lover and find yourself in Columbus, you absolutely have to check out the Book Loft of German Village, one of America's largest independent bookstores; it will become the catalyst for you getting lost in a book. No matter what time of the year, the lovely walkway to the entrance is enough to transport you to another world. Prepare to be amazed as you open the door. This historic building-turned-bookstore is an iconic stop in German Village, with 32 rooms filled with books on every topic imaginable. Creative organization makes it easy to navigate through the labyrinth of knowledge, and the selection of genres and styles is beyond impressive. If you are a true book lover, plan on spending a few hours here because it is nothing like you have ever seen.

Book Loft
631 S 3rd St., Columbus, 614-464-1774
bookloft.com

Stauf's Coffee
627 S 3rd St., Columbus, 614-221-1563
staufs.com

TIP
Arrive during Stauf's Coffee business hours to imbibe in a cup before your trip to book heaven.

OTHER BOOKSTORES

Dollar Book Swap
1723 Webster St., Dayton
thedollarbookswap.com

Loganberry Books
13015 Larchmere Blvd., Shaker Heights, 216-795-9800
loganberrybooks.com

The Learned Owl Book Shop
204 N Main St., Hudson, 330-653-2252
learnedowl.com

Fireside Book Shop
29 N Franklin St., Chagrin Falls, 440-247-4050
firesidebookshop.com

FIND BARGAINS
AT THE TANGER OUTLET MALL

Shopping at the Tanger Outlet Mall in Sunbury is an experience that promises both excitement and satisfaction. With its wide selection of stores and unbeatable discounts, this retail haven is a must-visit destination for shopaholics and bargain hunters alike. When you enter the mall, you are greeted with a vibrant atmosphere and a sense of anticipation. The open-air circular layout makes it easy to find the stores you are looking for. From fashion and accessories to home decor and electronics, there is something for everyone at this extensive shopping complex. Aside from the fantastic array of stores, the outlet mall also offers a range of amenities. Clean and spacious restrooms, comfortable seating areas, and ample parking facilities make navigating the mall hassle-free and enjoyable. Whether you are searching for a new wardrobe, home essentials, or the latest gadgets, the outlet mall in Sunbury is a shopping paradise that guarantees exceptional deals and a memorable experience.

400 S Wilson Rd., Sunbury, 740-965-2927
tanger.com/columbus

BROWSE
A HUGE FLEA MARKET

Bargain hunters and antique collectors will love the Hartville Marketplace & Flea Market. This sprawling marketplace is home to over 1,000 indoor and outdoor vendors who sell everything from vintage clothing and jewelry to unique home decor and handmade crafts. Visitors can spend hours browsing through the various stalls and booths, discovering hidden treasures and one-of-a-kind items. The indoor market is open year-round, with special events and promotions held throughout the year. One of the highlights of the Hartville Marketplace & Flea Market is its selection of locally sourced food and produce. From fresh baked goods and homemade jams to farm-fresh eggs and vegetables, there's something for everyone to enjoy. If you need a break from all the shopping, you can indulge in something from Sarah's Market Fresh Grill or the Coffee Mill. With its friendly vendors, diverse selection of goods, and lively atmosphere, it's no wonder why it's been a local favorite for over 80 years.

1289 Edison St. NW, Hartville, 330-877-9860

HANDPICK BLOOMS AND SHOP THE STALLS
AT THE PICKWICK PLACE

The Pickwick Place is a charming collection of beautifully renovated buildings that can be found on the outskirts of Bucyrus. This fantastic destination is home to a variety of exciting offerings, including the Market, the Stalls, the Cafe, and the Loft. If you're a foodie, start your visit at the Market, where you'll find a treasure trove of locally grown and sourced ingredients that are picked fresh and in season. Remember to bring a cooler to keep everything cool! Once you've stocked up, head over to the Cafe for a delicious snack or lunch. Here, almost everything is made to order and house-made, ensuring that your meal is fresh and delicious. Don't miss the Stalls, where you'll find an array of unique and interesting items that you simply can't find anywhere else. Shopping here will take a while because it is filled to the brim with local artisan goods.

1875 N Sandusky Ave., Bucyrus
The Market: 419-562-0683
The Loft: 419-408-6658
The Stalls: 419-689-5030
thepickwickplace.com

TIP
Visit during the U Pick Flower Fields' bloom to capture some Instagram-worthy shots. It's one of the most picturesque fields in Ohio.

PLUNGE YOURSELF
IN JAPANESE CULTURE

Discover the vibrant and eclectic culture of Japan at the Japan Marketplace. This one-of-a-kind destination boasts six unique Japanese shops, making it the perfect place to immerse yourself in all things Japanese. Whether you're looking for authentic Japanese cuisine or specialty grocery items, you're bound to find what you need at this marketplace. The gift shop is a must-visit for anyone interested in Japanese culture, as it offers a wide range of unique items that are difficult to find elsewhere. From traditional Japanese clothing and accessories to quirky and fun souvenirs, there's something for everyone at this shop. If you're looking for a sweet treat, stop by the French-inspired Japanese bakery. They offer a delicious selection of pastries and baked goods, all infused with traditional Japanese flavors. It's the perfect way to indulge in a little bit of both cultures. With six distinct shops all in one location, it's the ideal place to spend an afternoon browsing, shopping, sampling delicious food, and experiencing the magic of Japan right in the heart of Columbus.

1167 Old Henderson Rd., Columbus, 614-451-6002
japanmarketplace.com

RELIVE CHILDHOOD MEMORIES
WITH NOSTALGIC CANDIES

If you're looking for a candy store to satisfy your sweet tooth, b.a. Sweetie Candy Company is the place to go. With over 4,500 different types of candy and treats, there is something for everyone at this fantastic store. From classic favorites like gummy bears and chocolate bars to more unique options like sour gummies and Japanese candy, b.a. Sweetie has it all. One of the best things about stopping here often is that they constantly add new products to their shelves. Whether you're in the mood for something sweet and fruity or something rich and chocolatey, you're sure to find it. If you want to relive some childhood memories, this store has a great selection of nostalgic candies from your youth. From candy cigarettes to Pop Rocks, you'll feel like a kid again when you step through the doors. But b.a. Sweetie isn't just a candy store—they also have an ice cream shop. Place your order, then hop on one of the swinging chairs to enjoy.

6770 Brookpark Rd., Cleveland, 216-739-2244
sweetiescandy.com

DIG FOR TREASURE
AT AN ANTIQUE MALL

If you're an antique lover, then you simply can't miss the Heart of Ohio Antique Center. Located near Springfield, this antique mall is a treasure trove of vintage and antique items that will take you on a journey through time. With more than 650 vendors, you'll find everything from vintage clothing to antique furniture and rare collectibles. As soon as you step inside, you'll be transported to another era. The mall is sprawling, with aisle after aisle of antique shops and vendors. You'll be amazed by the sheer variety of items on offer, from antique jewelry to mid-century modern furniture. The Heart of Ohio Antique Center is the perfect place to spend a lazy afternoon. Find yourself lost in the nostalgia of it all, reminiscing about the past and marveling at the beauty of the vintage items on display. If you're looking for a unique shopping experience that will transport you back in time, look no further than the Heart of Ohio Antique Center.

4785 E National Rd., Springfield, 937-324-2188
heartofohioantiques.com

Lakeside Chautauqua in Lakeside, Ohio

MAIN STREETS
AND NEIGHBORHOODS

FIND LOCAL GOODS
AND HIDDEN GEMS

Beautiful Marysville is loved by visitors and locals alike, thanks to its iconic mix of small-town charm, lively uptown district, and steeped in history of locally grown and crafted products and uncommon experiences. The downtown area offers an array of charming shops and eateries, the beautifully restored Avalon Theatre, and the original hardware store of O. M. Scott, founder of the ScottsMiracle-Gro company. While visiting, don't miss Union Station 1820, a must-see destination for those searching for locally made and naturally crafted products courtesy of a multitude of talented artists and farmers. Venture outside of Marysville to discover an abundance of orchards, U-pick experiences, renowned wineries and breweries, and beloved covered bridges. Don't miss the opportunity to explore the more than eight farmers' markets that dot the pastoral landscape of Union County in summer and harvest season.

Union Station 1820
109 E 5th St., Marysville, 937-644-2899
unionstation1820.com

Avalon Theatre
121 S Main St., Marysville, 937-738-2032
theavalontheatre.org

O. M. Scott
119 S Main St., Marysville, 937-738-7238

TIP

Make sure while at Union Station 1820 to obtain information on the covered bridges and seek out naturally crafted attractions along the route.

HAVE
AN ALTOGETHER ADVENTURE

Grove City's historic downtown area is a delightful place filled with charming shops, tasty eateries, and stunning architecture. As you stroll through the streets, you can feel the town's rich culture and history seeping into your bones. While the buildings have been restored and preserved, they still offer visitors contemporary amenities while providing a glimpse into the past. You can create candles at the Chandler, sip on a coffee at Transcend Coffee, or browse through the local stores. Moreover, Grove City is home to two Columbus metro parks, which are home to a bison herd and backcountry campsites. You can also take a memorable kayak trip down the Big Darby Creek with Trapper John's Canoe Livery or engage in a fun paintball game at LVL UP Sports. History lovers will enjoy the historic Century Village and Grant-Sawyer Home. Plan a whole weekend and have an urban adventure.

Grove City Guide + Gear
3995 Broadway, Ste. 100, Grove City, 614-539-8747
visitgrovecityoh.com/attractions/grove-city-visitors-center

The Chandler
4048 Broadway, Grove City, 614-887-8381
thechandler.co

Transcend Coffee + Roastery
4050 Broadway, Grove City, 614-991-0911
facebook.com/transcendcoffeegc

LVL UP Sports
5390 Harrisburg Pike, Grove City, 614-313-1382
lvlupsports.com

Century Village
4185 Orders Rd., Grove City, 614-277-3061
grovecityohhistory.org/century-village

Grant-Sawyer Home
4126 Haughn Rd., Grove City, 614-277-3050
grovecityohhistory.org/grant-sawyer-home

LET YOUR
INNER HIPPIE OUT

If you're searching for a charming and distinctive town to visit, put Yellow Springs on your short list. This small town is renowned for its dynamic arts scene, independent shops, and delicious local cuisine, and is welcoming to all. Discover the beauty of Glen Helen Nature Preserve or John Bryan State Park, where you can hike through dense hardwood forests and enjoy stunning waterfalls. During the summer, be sure to attend the weekly farmers market, where you can sample fresh produce and handcrafted goods from local vendors. You won't want to miss out on the Yellow Springs Street Fair, which occurs annually and offers a groovy and uplifting experience. While you're here, stay at the Mills Park Hotel, a 28-room hotel modeled after the 19th-century home of William Mills, located within walking distance of downtown excitement and excellent dining options.

Yellow Springs Chamber of Commerce
101 Dayton St., Yellow Springs, 937-767-2686
yellowspringsohio.org

Glen Helen Nature Preserve
405 Corry St., Yellow Springs, 937-769-1902
glenhelen.org

John Bryan State Park
3790 State Rte. 370, Yellow Springs
ohiodnr.gov/go-and-do/plan-a-visit/find-a-property/
john-bryan-state-park

Mills Park Hotel
321 Xenia Ave., Yellow Springs, 937-319-0400
millsparkhotel.com

Yellow Springs Street Fair
yellowspringsohio.org/street-fair

VISIT
OHIO'S AMISH COUNTRY

If you're seeking simplicity, Ohio's Amish Country is the perfect destination for you. It's home to the state's largest Amish community and the charming village of Berlin. This quaint little town is right in the heart of Amish Country and boasts picturesque scenery and charming shops. It's an ideal place to escape the hustle and bustle of city life and unwind. Whether you're looking to relax or explore the rich history of the area, Berlin has something for everyone. You'll find a unique and authentic experience here that you won't find anywhere else. Don't miss dining at Boyd & Wurthmann, a staple since the 1930s; shopping at Sol's in Berlin with its three buildings filled with vendors; or visiting Sheiyah Market, a complex filled with home goods, a greenhouse, and a restored barn with high-end items.

Ohio's Amish Country
6 W Jackson St., Millersburg
330-674-3975, visitamishcountry.com

Sol's in Berlin
4914 W Main St., Berlin
330-893-3134, solsinberlin.com

Boyd & Wurthmann
4819 E Main St., Berlin
330-893-4000, boydandwurthmann.com

Sheiyah Market
4755 State Rte. 39, Berlin
330-893-2648, sheiyahmarket.com

TIP
If you want to learn more about the area, purchase Brandy Gleason's book, *100 Things to Do in Ohio's Amish Country Before You Die.*

HEAD OUT ON LAKE ERIE
TO CATCH WALLEYE

Are you ready to catch some fish? Look no further than Port Clinton, Ohio, the gateway to Lake Erie and the Walleye Capital of the World. As the sun rises over the eastern shore, boats set out for a day of fishing, with anglers from all corners of the globe dropping a line in the waters. The excitement builds with each cast as you eagerly await that telltale tug on your line. When you finally hook a feisty walleye, the rush of adrenaline is indescribable. Whether you opt for a private charter or join the headboat, you're guaranteed to have the time of your life.

As you head back to the dock, the sun sets over the western horizon, painting the sky with hues of red, orange, and gold. It's a picture-perfect end to an unforgettable day. Pack your gear, book your hotel, and get ready to limit out on Lake Erie.

Sassy Sal Headboat
40 Jefferson St., Port Clinton
sassysalcharters.com

Blue Sky Charters
937-414-6742
blueskycharters.net

Champion Charters
419-732-8195
championchartersoh.com

D.O.C charters
740-507-1266, Marblehead

TIP
Buy an Ohio fishing license in advance. Depending on the type of boat you choose, you may need to bring your own fishing gear.

DISCOVER THE CHARMING TOWN
OF BELLEFONTAINE

Bellefontaine is a charming small town tucked amid the rolling hills of Logan County, surrounded by picturesque parks and stunning scenery. This idyllic town is home to friendly people, historical landmarks like the oldest concrete street in Ohio, and exciting attractions that make it a must-visit destination for travelers seeking a relaxing escape. The town's rich history is evident in the local museums and galleries, which offer a glimpse into the past and present of this vibrant community. Stroll through the walkable downtown shopping area, where you'll find a plethora of locally owned shops and restaurants. Grab a coffee or a bite to eat and take your time drinking in the up-and-coming arts scene, which includes an impressive array of murals and public art installations. Don't forget to snap a picture at one of the colorful murals before getting a bite to eat at one of the many delicious restaurants in town, like pizza at Six Hundred Downtown or upscale dining at the Syndicate! Whether you're looking for a relaxing weekend getaway or an action-packed adventure, Bellefontaine is the perfect destination. So pack your bags and experience all this charming town has to offer; unexpected surprises await.

130 S Main St., B101, Bellefontaine
downtownbellefontaine.com

Six Hundred Downtown
108 S Main St., Bellefontaine, 937-599-6600
600downtown.com

The Syndicate
213 S Main St., Bellefontaine, 937-210-5165
syndicatedowntown.com

GO EXPLORE
OHIO'S BEST-KEPT SECRET

Time seems to slow down along the banks of the Ohio River where the town of Marietta has rooted itself. Wandering through the streets of Marietta, you are immediately struck by the architectural splendor that graces every corner. Victorian-era homes with intricate detailing stand proudly, a testament to the town's storied past. The quaint downtown is lined with charming boutiques, art galleries, and cozy cafés, inviting you to explore and discover hidden treasures like the ones you'll find at Schafer Leather Store, owned and operated by five generations of the Schafer family. Stay in the historic Lafayette Hotel, which boasts stunning views of the skyline and river, and sleep where history was made. Marietta is a town steeped in rich history and proudly wears the title of the first permanent settlement in the Northwest Territory. Its historic sites and landmarks serve as a living testament to its past.

Marietta and Washington County CVB
mariettaohio.org

Schafer Leather Store
140 Front St., Marietta
740-373-5101
schaferleather.com

Historic Lafayette Hotel
101 Front St., Marietta
740-373-5522
lafayettehotel.com

TIP
Visit during the annual Ohio River Sternwheel Festival, with its majestic riverboats and vibrant fireworks display.

ACTIVITIES
BY SEASON

SPRING

SUMMER

FALL

WINTER

SUGGESTED
ITINERARIES

DATE NIGHT

Savor History in the Oldest Continuously Operated Business in Ohio, 20

Hop Aboard a Dinner Train for an Evening of Elegance, 64

Celebrate Tradition and Fine Dining at the Pine Club, 14

Get Away to the Italian-Inspired Gervasi Vineyard, 44

Sing Along with the Entertainers at a Dinner Theater, 39

FOR YOUNGER CHILDREN

Discover the Ohio State Fair, 32

Entertain the Kids While They Learn, 58

Indulge in Ice Cream at an Iconic Dairy, 10

Get Wild at the Columbus Zoo, 36

FOR TEENS

Experience Thrills at the Roller Coaster Capital of the World, 34

Sample the Best Doughnuts in Ohio, 12

Have an Altogether Adventure, 158

Unleash Your Inner Foodie at Odd Fodder, 24

• •

• •

INDEX

• •